MW00775508

THE NOVOGRATZ
CHRONICLES

To Adelle

Happy Reading!

Cortney Novogratz

Robert Novogratz

THE NOVOGRATZ CHRONICLES

Lessons Learned from Twenty-Five Years of Buying and Renovating Houses

Cortney and Robert Novogratz

PA PRESS

PRINCETON ARCHITECTURAL PRESS · NEW YORK

To
Wolfgang
Bellamy
Tallulah
Breaker
Five
Holleder
and
Major

This book is for all of you—
for your curiosity and adaptability,
your laughter and your generous spirits,
your talents and your resilience.
We've lived in many, many homes by now,
but the truth is, you are our home,
no matter our address.

"

Art resides in
the quality of doing;
process is not magic.

—Charles Eames

"

First love is only a
little foolishness and
a lot of curiosity.

—George Bernard Shaw

Contents

Foreword 8

Introduction 11

1   **IGNORANCE IS BLISS** 21

2   **EMBRACE THE CHAOS** 43

3   **WRECK OF THE CENTURY** 65

4   **COUNTRY COMFORT** 91

5   **ROBBING PETER TO PAY PAUL** 113

6   **ROOM WITH A (HIGHWAY) VIEW** 139

—

REALITY TV 161

—

7   **CRYSTALS, DUNE BUGGIES, AND LEARNING TO WORK WITH WHAT YOU'VE GOT** 175

8   **HOORAY FOR HOLLYWOOD!** 197

9   **NEVER (EVER) TAKE YOUR EYE OFF THE BALL** 223

10   **THE PINK HOUSE** 245

Acknowledgments 269

About the Authors 270

Foreword / Ree Drummond

I first "met" Cortney and Robert like many of their other fans did—by watching *9 by Design* on Bravo years ago. I was immediately captivated by this cool design duo with seven adorable kids and jaw-dropping talent. When they reached out to me some time later and offered to redo my daughters' bedroom as part of their HGTV show, I was more than a little starstruck—not to mention *intimidated* by the idea that the glamorous TV couple would be walking through the door of our then not-so-glamorous (and very lived-in) Oklahoma home.

You can imagine my surprise when Southern-drawled Cortney and charmingly casual Robert turned out to be the kindest, most generous souls, and we became instant friends. They brought along their twin daughters on that design trip, and my four kids clicked with them right away. It was the sweetest week, and it ended with my girls getting the bedroom of their dreams. However, the design project, as incredible as it was, turned out to be almost secondary to the genuine connections we formed. Our families still keep in touch after all these years, and we just love the whole Novogratz crew.

Cortney and Robert are a magical, dynamic force, and this book is a first-person tour through the remarkable path they have forged together as designers, innovators, and fearless risk takers over the past thirty years. From renovating their first Chelsea townhouse as a young couple to navigating the world of reality TV to creating havens for their family in the Berkshires and Brazil to countless other passion projects (including a castle in Los Angeles and Waverly, their current family home-sweet-home in NYC), you will love hearing about the behind-the-scenes planning, collaboration, passion, and absolute grit it took to get each one done. Cortney and Robert's thought process is fascinating to observe, and if you love to read about renovation and design—or even just what it takes to be a day-in, day-out entrepreneur—you are in for an absolute treat. Just a heads-up, though: this book will spark ideas and may give you the itch to find an old building to redo!

As you read about their adventures and accomplishments (and even their challenges and obstacles), you'll see that Cortney and Robert are driven by curiosity, determination, and the desire to create something beautiful out of nothing. They live in a world of possibilities, and that energy is so inspiring. I think what I loved most was seeing the natural push and pull of their relationship and how they'd trust each other from one project to the next, even if one of them wasn't fully on board to begin with. That, and their ever-present love for their family, gave this book its beautiful heart. I know it will inspire anyone who reads it.

Robert and Cortney playing in the brick archway of the kitchen

INTRODUCTION

[Robert: roman text]

It's New York City, 1995. The world is a very different place than it is today, and the city is almost another universe entirely.

Yellow taxis still rule the streets (pedestrians be damned), you still need tokens to ride the subway, and bike lanes are unheard of. Smoking in public places? It was only recently banned in New York bars, but you're free to light up almost anyplace else. Times Square still has triple-X movie theaters, and CBGB is an actual punk club, not just a place to buy T-shirts. Bill Clinton is president, O. J. Simpson is on trial, and Rudy Giuliani is just a year into his first term as New York mayor.

Manhattan was right on the cusp between the borough it'd been—violent, dirty, exciting—and the borough it was becoming—still exciting and a little dirty, but not as violent. The murder rate in New York plunged in 1995 to its lowest level in twenty-five years. But the city still had an edge to it. You could still visit the Meatpacking District and remember why it got its name.

This was the city that Cortney and I moved to. We weren't natives, but we loved everything about New York—the grit, the adrenaline, the utter lack of sleeping. We were young, but that wasn't the reason we regularly stayed up till dawn. The city demanded it. There was so much to see, so much to discover. You couldn't just stay at home and watch all the action from a computer. If you didn't get outside and look for what was happening, you'd miss it all.

So when we decided in 1995 that the time was right to buy our first home, we did it the only way we knew how—by walking. There was no Zillow, and no smartphones to help us find our way around the city and explore neighborhoods and properties. We'd pick up a copy of the *New York Times* or the *Village Voice*, scour the real estate section until we got super depressed because we couldn't afford anything, then hit the streets in search of for-sale signs until yet another day ended in despair. There just wasn't much in our budget. But we kept walking, buying cheap coffee for extra energy at the neighborhood delis (there wasn't a Starbucks on every corner or fancy coffee places).

It was an amazing way to discover New York. We never knew what we'd find next. Was our dream home out there somewhere? Our phones wouldn't tell us. Our phone was back home, in our tiny apartment, connected to the wall like everybody else's. The only way we would find that perfect home was to keep walking and keep looking up, toward the horizon. Because in 1995, what waited around every corner was always another surprise.

[Cortney: semibold text]

Okay, so maybe we should back up. In hindsight, it seems inevitable that Robert and I ended up in New York.

Growing up in southern Georgia, I always felt like a New Yorker. There was just something about the city that I loved. All I knew about it was what I saw in the movies, and I'm sure I idealized it in my head. I don't remember this, but my sisters swear that when I was little, I'd have tea parties with my dolls that would end with me saying, "Okay, bye, meet me in New York City at 8 p.m." When I was a teenager, my family took a trip to the city, and I was so enamored with it that I told my parents, "You can just leave me here." There was just something about New York that felt like I belonged there. The pulse, the energy. I've never felt more at home anywhere else in the world.

Thankfully, I didn't jump on a bus bound for Manhattan the moment I graduated from high school. I went to college in Florida, and in 1992, as my senior year was coming to a close, I drove up to Charlotte, North Carolina, to visit my older sister Brandi, who was soon moving out of the country. I came to help her pack and attend her going-away party. I was just twenty at the time, practically a baby. I didn't know anybody at the party, but I noticed this tall, handsome guy across the room.

I didn't go to that party to meet anyone, much less find a boyfriend. But he sparked my curiosity. He clearly wasn't Southern—the Talking Heads T-shirt gave that away—so he stood out in the sea of Southern men all dressed like they were on their way to play golf. Also, at six foot four, he *literally* stood out. He was tall and lanky and carried himself a little differently than the other guys I knew.

"You're sweating a lot," I told him. Yes, that was my opening line. Then I asked him if I made him nervous.

He smirked at me. "No, I'm just hot."

We talked for a bit. I learned that he lived in Charlotte, was a stockbroker, and seemed to be doing quite well for himself. But he was restless. He told me he wasn't sure if he wanted to stay in North Carolina for the rest of his life, and he mentioned that most of his siblings were migrating to New York City, where his grandmother lived.

He was a homeowner. He'd bought his first house in Charlotte at twenty-five, a young age, and I was impressed with how much he talked about his home and love of home, which I identified with. And while Robert had bought a five-thousand-square-foot house for $79,000, he'd invited three friends to become roommates and help him pay the mortgage.

When I told him I was going to move to New York right after graduation and had my sights on being an actress or a model, he

Cortney and Robert in the early days

smirked again and said, "You're a little short to be a model. Maybe you should stick to acting."

I replied, "If I was taller, I'd be a supermodel, and I wouldn't be standing here talking to you."

Later, he told me that it wasn't so much love at first sight as love at first comeback.

One thing led to another, and we found ourselves making out. My sister caught us and instantly recognized Robert. "That's the guy I was telling you about!" she exclaimed.

Six months earlier, Brandi had met Robert at a party, and she was convinced we were made for each other. "He was like the male version of you," she told me. I didn't ask for his name because I couldn't have been less interested. Why would I want to date some random dude from Charlotte? I was moving to New York City to follow my dreams. Well, I guess fate had other ideas.

We stayed together for two days, just talking and getting to know each other, dreaming of what our lives together might look like.

Turns out, we had more in common than simply wanting to leave the South and seek something else. Robert came from a military family, and his parents had moved him and his six siblings several times, all over the country, until they finally settled down in Alexandria, Virginia, where he spent most of his youth. Growing up,

Robert worked all different kinds of jobs—from having a newspaper route to waiting tables at seventeen years old at restaurants in Old Town Alexandria. I'd likewise grown up in a big family and worked all my life (my mother and father owned car washes throughout the South), so we shared some pretty important values that would come to work in our favor.

We started dating long-distance, which was not easy, but we knew we'd end up in New York together that fall. Robert found a rent-controlled prewar apartment on West End Avenue. It was huge, with two bedrooms, at an extremely great, borderline-insane price. I would rather have stayed with him, but my parents weren't thrilled about me living with a man I wasn't married to, so I found a little place down on the East Side to call my own.

Robert was working in finance, and I was going to acting classes, waiting tables, and auditioning. I auditioned for a soap opera; I got a small Mercedes commercial; I was in a play. It was dribs and drabs, but it paid the bills. And it was a great way to explore the city. We weren't just sticking to a three-block radius, going to the same bars and restaurants and clubs every night. We were venturing into neighborhoods all over the city and getting to know it like a new friend.

I got a bartending job in the Meatpacking District, which at the time was not the safest place to venture after dark. Soon after, one of my girlfriend got a gig as a cigarette girl at this place called the Vault, which was just around the corner from my bar, at Fourteenth Street and Ninth Avenue. Neither of us had had any idea what went on there until she came home after her first shift and reported, "Yeah, it's an S-M club. The whole place is built like a dungeon, and everybody's in bondage gear, cracking whips and locking each other in cages." Suddenly, something came into focus for me. "I'm always serving people dressed head to toe in leather. You don't think…?" And she replied, "Of *course* that's where they're going."

I was a little naive, but even during those early months as a New Yorker, I was never intimidated. I certainly had struggles, especially financially in the beginning, but the city never felt hostile or unwelcoming. It was exciting and fast-paced, and the only place on Earth I wanted to be. It's where the best of the best lived and worked, from fashion to finance, from publishing to theater—you name it, they were all on this island called Manhattan doing amazing things. We wanted to be doing something unique and noteworthy. We just weren't sure what yet. But what better place to find ourselves than New York, where there is always someone smarter than you, better looking than you, richer than you? That might sound intimidating, but to Robert and me, it was invigorating. When the bar is that high, you have no choice but to jump with everything you've got.

Cortney eventually moved in with me after her apartment burned down. The likely cause, according to the fire department, was an electrical short. And thankfully, she wasn't there when it happened—she was with me, cohosting a big party, which was one of the ways we brought in income. Afterward it just made sense for her to move in with me.

Soon after, we started talking about marriage and looking for a place of our own. We both wanted a big family, so that was definitely a consideration. Some of our friends had recently moved to the suburbs and encouraged us to join them. Many of them lived in lovely places, but we'd just gotten to Manhattan and had no plans to leave anytime soon. After many months of looking at expensive apartments and lofts and co-ops, we came up with the crazy idea of trying to buy a townhouse. We'd found out that a single-family home was less expensive than a condo or a loft in many cases.

So, how do you find your first home when it's 1995 and you're still relatively new to a city and the internet is still in its infancy? We just started walking. We walked until our feet ached. There wasn't a block we didn't march down, looking for anything for sale in our price range. Most of the townhouses in New York City we came upon were in Greenwich Village, Chelsea, or Harlem. In Greenwich

Village, townhouses were around a million each, and Chelsea was half that, Harlem even less. We went back and forth between Chelsea and Harlem, and finally decided to go with Chelsea, as we were falling in love with downtown Manhattan. We decided we wanted a townhouse, no matter how long it took, and Chelsea was where we were going to get one—a proper home, smack dab in the middle of our adopted city, a short walk to everything.

Chelsea was a predominantly gay neighborhood, extremely colorful, a melting pot of eccentricity and possibility. It was an urban ecosystem that could contain the Empire Diner on Tenth Avenue; the Chelsea Court Meat Market on Ninth Avenue and Twentieth Street, an old-school shop where the butcher, with his thick mustache and Brooklyn accent, knew all the customers by name and their favorite cuts of meat; and the Chelsea Hotel on Twenty-Third, home to punk rockers and Beat poets.

It was everything weird and eclectic and wonderful about the city, thriving and vibrant. Chelsea was gritty, just like the rest of downtown Manhattan—we saw potential there, and it was affordable for us. After living on the Upper West Side, we felt like downtowners at heart. Were we smart or just lucky? Probably a little of both. Luck certainly played into our buying at the bottom of the New York real estate market.

Through our countless walks around the neighborhood, we began to appreciate its grit and see the beauty in both the history of the area and its potential. The future Chelsea Market was still just an abandoned Nabisco building, controlled by sex workers and the site of several bloody gangland-style murders. But Chelsea was also a place where both a hidden Tibetan Buddhist monastery (a Sixteenth Street brick townhouse that included a throne for the Dalai Lama) and a hidden gay dance hall (the Roxy on Eighteenth Street near the West Side Highway, which served as a roller-skating rink by day) could flourish simultaneously.

Home to Irish and German immigrants who lived among a growing Latino population and ate out at Cuban and Cuban Chinese restaurants, Chelsea was founded by a British captain (who named the neighborhood after a veterans' hospital in London's Chelsea) and was developed by his grandson Clement Clarke Moore, who also wrote the beloved classic *The Night before Christmas* and basically invented Santa Claus.

It was truly a wild and a special place.

When we stumbled onto Nineteenth Street, that's when we found it—the building that would become our first home. At least from the outside, it wasn't anything special. Most people wouldn't have looked twice at it. It was an ugly duckling on an otherwise unremarkable street. But Cortney and I didn't just see what it was. We saw what it could become. We saw our future.

"What do you think?" I asked her.

"It's awful," she said. "I love it. Let's buy it."

So we did. And that's when our adventure began.

Thirty years and seven kids later, it's been a joy to relive where we've been and how far we've come—the blind chances we've taken, the inexplicable luck that has come our way, the great times we've had as a result of our hard work, and the challenging times we thought we'd never recover from.

Each of our projects has been unique and pushed us to grow in different ways. Some have been more successful creatively, some financially, some both (unsurprisingly, those are the ones we're most proud of).

While it rarely works to learn from others' mistakes, we hope you'll find something of your own dreams—both fulfilled and yet to be—in these pages. No matter what endeavors you're investing your time and energy in, whether it's renovating houses, selling real estate, getting a fledgling business off the ground, building an art career—whatever it is, we hope you'll find inspiration to get started, keep going, and have as much fun as possible along the way! We can say with confidence, looking back, that the hard times weren't as hard as we then thought, and the good times were even better.

We all know it goes fast, yet writing this book has made us realize that life goes by even faster than one can imagine. So we always try to express our gratitude at every turn for those who've helped us, and return the favor to those who are just starting out, while also enjoying the ride and the people who are on it with us. Like we've always told our kids: if you can do what you love with people you love *and* pay the bills, that's a pretty good gig. And believe it or not, we're just getting started.

Family portrait, 2010

Single-room occupancy only

1995

1

IGNORANCE IS BLISS
West Nineteenth Street
Chelsea, New York

"Only in New York"—it's a phrase we've all heard so often, it's become a cliché. But Chelsea in the early 1990s deserved that cliché. It *embodied* that cliché. As it so happens, it also applied to me and Cortney. What was to come on Nineteenth Street—our first home together as a married couple, our first child, our first foray into learning everything we didn't know about renovation, construction, and rehabbing a townhouse (which was pretty much everything!)—could *only* have happened in New York, and, more specifically, in Chelsea.

There were no young families living in Chelsea at that time. Robert and I planned to change that.

When we first met Joe, the owner of our future townhouse, he was sitting on the front stoop, looking like a tough-guy character from a Martin Scorsese film. Stocky, with thick hands, an impeccable dresser, he also wore a healthy amount of cologne. A first-generation Puerto Rican, he'd spent his entire life in the city, making a brief go of it as a pro boxer but quitting after one too many knockouts. Though he considered himself an artist (he was both a gourmet chef and a connoisseur of French cinema), he'd spent years in construction and dabbled in real estate. He was New York City friendly, meaning he was a straight shooter—a nice guy but with suspicions, and he was definitely suspicious of us. And could you blame him?

We were a young couple with big dreams and zero real estate experience. At the time, there was no mass migration of young people to the city—or to *anywhere*, really—buying and redoing property. It was, as far as we could tell, unheard of. Other couples we knew were buying move-in-ready houses, not old homes boarded up with plywood, their walls covered in graffiti, that needed to be gutted and rebuilt. So Joe had every reason to be wary, but after much back-and-forth, he agreed to hear us out. He'd begrudgingly taken a liking to us, and the feeling was mutual.

In early 1990, he'd paid just over a million dollars for that townhouse. No small chunk of change back then, but it still didn't seem that risky of an investment. Real estate in Manhattan was hotter than ever. It jumped a staggering 600 percent between 1977 and 1987 thanks to the Wall Street brokers with money to burn. But the bubble was short-lived. Just a month after Joe bought his townhouse, a recession put an end to the real estate renaissance, especially in New York. To make matters worse, his new property, upon purchase, came with a tenant who declined to vacate. Four years and tens of thousands in legal fees later, the squatter was finally gone, but Joe was left with a building whose value was sinking every day, looked straight out of post–World War II Europe, and had not attracted a single buyer in three years. Joe was sure it was cursed. He'd paid too much, the market was DOA, and he wanted to be done with it.

Enter me and Cortney.

His asking price was a little under half of what he'd paid. Once we got inside, flashlights in hand, we realized why. There was extensive fire and water damage, holes in the ceilings, and trash everywhere, and it reeked of mildew and rotting wood. And the floor plan made absolutely no sense: the main floor had been divided into eight tiny individual rooms with a single communal bathroom.

That's the first thing I noticed when we walked in—that we were standing in what felt like a hedge maze made up of little separate cubicles. It was slightly dizzying. In the night, you might not be entirely sure where the exit was in case of an emergency. Given that this was where we ostensibly wanted to live and raise a family, it was slightly terrifying.

But we noticed more than just the crumbling wood, the unmistakable scurrying of vermin, and the illogical, nefarious design. We saw the regal double doors that divided the house from the entryway, which made the place feel like an aging mansion. We saw the faded Hong Kong–red staircase with detailed moldings that curved slowly and elegantly up to the second floor. The house had beautiful old doors and high ceilings. I could see so clearly the grandness that had once been.

We asked to go upstairs to the second and third floors, but Joe said it was too dangerous in the dark—he didn't know how reliable the floors were. I begged him to let us look anyway, promising we wouldn't sue if one of us fell through the ceiling, which didn't seem outside the realm of possibility. He finally agreed. Not surprisingly, the upstairs was more of the same. It had been, at some point in its life, turned into an SRO (single-room occupancy). That's why it had been chopped into a bunch of tiny bedrooms and a bathroom. It was obvious why the place wasn't selling, despite all its Old World–ish charms.

After that first tour, we met up again with Joe at his Tribeca apartment to discuss details. He was warming to us and even shared his own plans for rehabbing the place, rolling out blueprints that he was clearly proud of. Though I didn't say it out loud, I knew at a glance that what he had in mind was not going to work for us.

In some ways, this is when our rehab of the property began. Even though the building wasn't yet ours, I was already redrawing the plans in my mind, making wish lists, imagining myself and Robert and our future family in our new home, our new city, our new life.

When we told friends and family what we were considering, they were, more or less, horrified. Nobody said, "That sounds like a fun challenge!" or "Go for it!" They said things like "Absolutely not." "You're throwing money away." "It's too close to the projects." "You can't afford to rebuild it." And on and on . . . All of which was true, by the way. Not only did we not have the money for a proper rehab, we barely had the financing to buy it at all. But for us, that was the reason to buy it. Things that might have given a more rational person pause—the crime in the neighborhood, the strange and wonderful mix of its residents, the influx of artists living on the cheap—were what made this risky and momentous plan so appealing.

Chelsea and all its history, its teeming creative pace, its hopeful gritty energy, had everything of the New York we'd fallen in love with. Give us your tired, your poor, your huddled masses who want to open art galleries where industry once reigned, who want to make art that will hang on the walls inside those galleries, and who, like us, want to live on a block full of more ethnicities than any other in the United States. The same block where our gay friends danced until dawn in an old bowling alley, wearing skin-tight leather shorts if they wanted, and fitting right in.

The writing was definitely on the wall of the neighborhood we hoped to call home. The downtown art scene that had been thriving in SoHo was migrating north and west into Chelsea. A Chelsea that still had art and cheap coffee and the McBurney YMCA, of which I was a member, still famous for being featured in the video for the Village People's iconic song. The same Chelsea that had a new sports and entertainment complex in the works that would restore and revive the ailing historic Chelsea Piers along the Hudson River, offering a range of

Early demo days

recreation opportunities, including waterfront access. A Chelsea in which there were whispers of a retail and food complex known as the Chelsea Market that bordered on the Meatpacking District. This was a Chelsea of competing interests and exciting contradictions, serving a range of Manhattanites, including families like we hoped to have. We loved it. And we wanted to stay.

Our only issue was money—not an uncommon issue when it comes to bringing a vision into reality. Unfortunately, a disarming smile and lots of giddy enthusiasm were not going to buy us a building, even in the rock-bottom New York real estate market of the mid-1990s. I'd recently gotten a signing bonus from a new job, and I had some savings from over the years. We could manage a down payment, and maybe after merging what was left with the bank loan we hoped to get, we could afford the renovations. We hoped that our belief in what we were doing would carry us just far enough to make it work. We didn't know what we didn't know, but we had a vision we refused to give up on.

When we shared our plan with Joe, he told us no bank would consider giving us a loan for a condemned building. It'd be like throwing cash into a bonfire. And if we did by some chance get financial backing, the place needed far, far more than just a fresh coat of paint. It needed a serious gut job, closer to a complete transformation than a mere facelift. It needed everything that we were completely unqualified to do.

We didn't want to believe him. So the next morning I called Gary, a guy we knew at the bank who'd helped us up to that point with comparatively trivial issues—lost ATM cards, bounced checks, and the like. When we told him what we wanted to do with this house—basically a dump that everyone with any sense in New York real estate had passed over with extreme prejudice—he laughed, then told us he couldn't help and referred us to a few others who would end up saying the same.

So although on paper nothing about our situation made sense, we had an idea. We asked Joe to meet us at the Big Cup—a favorite café in the heart of Chelsea famous for its gay pickup scene, where the cups were as big as a soup bowl—and begged for more time. "Listen, we're screwed," I told him. "You were right. There's no way a bank is giving us a loan. If we use everything in our nest egg to pay your asking price and buy it outright, we'll have nothing left to rehab with. We'll be a couple of suckers living in a house that's falling down around us with vermin and tiny rooms, totally unlivable. But we absolutely love the place and we can see what's possible there. Everything that's wrong with it, we can see how to make right." We asked Joe for ninety days to find more financing—from family? from friends? We didn't know. But we wanted more time to figure it out.

Joe got mad. Really mad. Not at us so much as at the situation. He was so close to finally unburdening his money pit of a building, and we were asking him to wait while we tried to do the impossible and raise a lot of cash in a short period of time. We all sat there in silence for what felt like an hour, but was probably only a couple of minutes, when he abruptly offered up a question that would change everything: "Do you know what 'taking paper' means?"

We had no idea.

"Taking paper is a way to purchase a gut job without involving a bank."

Of course, my first thought was, "Uh-oh. Are we in Scorsese territory again?" Even the phrase "taking paper" sounded shady. What was he proposing exactly?

Joe explained: we'd make a small down payment on the town-house, and the rest would be treated as a loan from him—an interest-only loan. He would basically hold on to the mortgage until we paid him in full. It was an unbelievable deal—which, as far as we could tell, involved zero horses' heads left in our bed.

We were interested, of course, but also a little wary. What's that old adage? If something seems too good to be true, it probably is. We asked how much time we'd have to pay him back. "Three years," he said. "And if you can't get it renovated and a loan from the bank at

"

One of the great aphorisms for living a more peaceful life turns out to also work for rehabbing a 150-year-old house for the first time: keep your eyes on what you have to do *today*.

that point—which you absolutely should be able to, if you know what you're doing—" (we weren't going to tell him that we didn't have a clue what we were doing) "I'll take it all. The house, the down payment, and the interest."

Three years? How hard could that be?

It was an incredible opportunity, but one where we could potentially lose everything—not just the house, but every last cent we put into it—if we fumbled. And any oddsmaker, given our track record, or rather a complete lack of a record in this area, would've said the same thing: good luck! Because the odds aren't just stacked against you; they are stacked, cemented, and sealed. Gary's advice was simple: "Don't do it." I believe he even said, "I'm *begging* you not to do it."

We told Joe we needed to think about it, which was a lie. Of course we were going to say yes. What was the alternative?

We could have walked away and not taken the ginormous risk. Most of our friends, dating or newly married, were moving out of the city into Westchester or the Jersey suburbs. Our family and friends— people who really cared about us—tried steering us in an easier, safer direction: "The suburbs are affordable. They're easy. You won't lose everything trying to finance a crumbling house that the banks won't touch." They weren't wrong, but Robert and I had been in the city for almost three years, dating, working, having fun hosting and producing parties, and now our Georgia wedding was on the horizon. We were meeting more and more people, growing in confidence both as a couple and in our respective skill sets—Robert as an event producer and me as a designer. Despite how little we knew about the practicalities of this kind of project, we did know some important things. We knew each other. And we knew, though we couldn't say *how* we knew it, that if we could just get our own building in the city, our own home, we could carve out a life that worked for us.

In other words, we knew what we wanted. We wanted *this* house on *this* block in *this* neighborhood in *this* city. Joe gave us three days to make a decision, and the night before his deadline, Robert and I talked. Do you remember what you told me?

I do. "I don't think Joe respects us, but he wants to unload this house. And for whatever reason, he wants to unload it on us." Maybe he was charmed by us. Maybe he thought we could actually do something cool with it. That we were sufficiently stubborn and determined to pull it off. He'd come out ahead either way. You don't want to make a deal with someone who *wants* to see you fail. But it might not be the worst idea to make a deal with someone who doesn't necessarily care if you fail because he has nothing to lose.

If we took the risk, we'd also get the autonomy we wanted. We wouldn't have a business partner showing up every day asking for updates, demanding progress reports, nitpicking our choices. We could do the house our way. Sink or swim, it was on us.

So the deal we eventually struck with Joe turned out to be our only option. The contract—or, rather, "purchase agreement"—was almost laughably simple. There wasn't the usual ninety-day waiting period for loan approvals and title searches and mortgage insurance. We just showed up at Joe's lawyer's office with a checkbook and watched as Joe wrote up, by hand, a two-page legal document. It cut right to the chase, in plain language: that day, we'd deliver a down payment for the privilege of restoring Joe's property, in which we'd invest what remained of our money. If, after three years, we weren't able to hand over the remainder plus interest to Joe, everything would forfeit back to him: the house, the deposit, all of it.

Signing that agreement could have terrified us. But it didn't. It was exhilarating. Up to that point, we'd admittedly still felt like kids, new at taking care of our grown-up lives, but with one signature, everything changed. We were *homeowners*. We were on our way.

Now came the difficult part—or the fun part, depending on which day you asked: hiring the team. We began the only way we knew how, by finding friends with any experience in construction and asking (sometimes begging) for advice.

My college roommate's dad was a contractor in Queens, and he agreed to come out and look at the house, maybe give us a few pointers. He showed up and immediately started peppering us with questions: How are you gonna heat the house? How are you gonna cool the house? Do you have a plan for the electrical and plumbing? Do you have a contractor insurance indemnification form? The list went on and on with things we hadn't considered or heard of and/ or didn't know how to solve, and I got completely overwhelmed. Robert and I didn't have the answers. But I knew that if I allowed myself to get intimidated by what I didn't know, I was done for. So I took a breath, looked at my friend's dad, and said, "I don't know, but we're going to figure it out."

And that's exactly what we did. Sometimes all it takes is the willingness to show up and learn something new every day. If you look too long and too hard at the big picture, it's easy to get over-whelmed. One of the great aphorisms for living a more peaceful life turns out to also work for rehabbing a 150-year-old house for the first time: keep your eyes on what you have to do *today*. What do I need to know and learn to solve today's problem?

We reached out to our friend Doug, an engineer who'd gone to school with one of Robert's brothers. A very sweet guy. He's always reminded me of Richie Cunningham from *Happy Days*. That kind of sweet. We asked if he'd come take a look at the place, just to get his thoughts on how deep the hole was that we were going to be climbing out of. He agreed that the place was in terrible shape but that the structure and foundation were sound. In other words, it had good bones.

Actually, I think his exact words were, "The foundation seems sound enough, but you might want to run some tests." We heard "seems sound enough" and then just stopped listening. That was good enough for us. He may as well have said, "You're good to go!"

Doug's second suggestion was that we find an architect with a working knowledge of "interior rendering" as well as construction laws and regulations. "Meet with at least three architects and get three bids. Then take the middle bid," the theory being that the cheapest bid would likely come from the least talented architect, and the most expensive from an architect overestimating their worth. The middle bidder was generally the best choice—the one with enough confidence not to undervalue themself but humble enough not to charge top dollar.

The budget in our head was five, maybe ten grand at most for the whole deal. But the first architect we met with walked into the house, looked around, and announced, "I can do this for fifty grand, no problem." We figured that that was the "high bid" guy. Turns out, we were wrong.

During one of our interviews with another architect, we realized yet again how little we could afford. After asking our set of ready-made questions, Cortney asked the question we were both thinking: "How much would you charge us for just measuring the house?"

"Twelve thousand dollars," he said, like he'd be giving us a deal.

Twelve grand *just to measure the house*? That was our entire kitchen budget!

We thanked him politely for his time and said we'd think about it. After he left, we walked to the nearest hardware store and bought a measuring tape. Total price: $2.99. Savings: $11,997.01. Already we were slashing our budget.

The next day, we met with two more guys, from an uptown architecture firm. We were young, but they were younger. Meticulously clean, well groomed, and *very* well dressed, they wore their expertise like they wore their Prada—they were pros who had never had so much as a sprinkling of sawdust on them. We've learned through the years that it's not as important to have expensive experts on your team as it is to have people who get their hands dirty, believe in you, and are willing to collaborate.

As we led them through the house, they nodded and wrinkled their noses like they were taking in and processing the potential work ahead. We barely made it past the kitchen and they were already giving us advice. Everything was urgent and had to be done *right away*. In other words, if we waited too long to put them on the payroll, the house was going to collapse into a mushroom cloud of dust. We asked questions, and it was clear they knew their stuff. We didn't doubt their skills—they were certified architects, after all—but did they have on-site construction experience? Had they spent time out from behind their desks? They veered away from our questions about how their experience would transfer to this particular project. More important, though, their approach at taking on a potential new client left a lot to be desired. It was as if they were trying to scare us into hiring them, and they believed it was actually going to work.

By the time we got up to the second floor, I was genuinely pissed about all of it: how they were talking to us, how they were trying to pressure us into taking out the checkbook, being vague about what exactly they were bringing to the table. Without thinking it through, I abruptly interrupted one of them as he spoke with great aplomb about the second-floor bathroom. What came out of my mouth sounded, at first, like a sarcastic threat: "What if we just did it without an architect?" Apparently I'd uttered the unthinkable, but continued: "Why do we actually *need* an architect to renovate a brownstone if there won't be any significant structural changes?"

They laughed. "You can't be serious," one of them said, raising his eyebrows.

And I realized I actually was.

But we were wise enough to know that we needed other people to complete our vision, even if we didn't have the money to do it the way we "should." We also couldn't finish the entire house with just the two of us and a measuring tape, as tempting as that sounded. So we kept on interviewing people—contractors, engineers, carpenters, anybody who could hold a hammer or owned a T-square—partly to find the talent we needed to do the jobs we couldn't figure out ourselves, and partly to get a crash course in home rehab.

Every time we coaxed a professional to come check out our house, it provided more evidence that we were in over our heads. "You're building with wood?" they'd ask, disbelievingly. "Nobody does that anymore. The place'll burn down." But even when they caught us red-handed trying to act like professionals when we so clearly weren't, we still managed to turn everything into a teaching moment. One moment they were warning us against using wood, and the next they were showing us how to use auger bits to drill through the studs to run wires through wood-framed walls.

The lesson? Don't be afraid to ask questions, and listen hard to the answers. People will teach you almost anything if you show some curiosity about their expertise. Being eager to learn goes a long way.

In our case, we accommodated the experts. We welcomed them. We'd give the person a tour and say, "Tell us about *your* vision. What do *you* think this house needs? Where would *you* start?" They'd start explaining their ideas and we'd nod along, writing everything down. "Interesting! And what's 'egress' again?"

Putting our ragtag team together was part intuition and part New York City magic—family members, friends of family members, folks we met at parties. The universe conspired, and before we knew it, we'd assembled an eclectic team who were ready and excited for the challenge:

AARON, GENERAL CONTRACTOR

The twenty-two-year-old boyfriend of Robert's older sister's best friend was pitched to us as an experienced carpenter—"a young Hemingway with rugged hands and incredible talent." Although he showed up looking like a college kid in tattered shorts and Birkenstocks, he became the central member of our team.

MARIE, EXPEDITING AND DRAFTING

She not only had the skills to draw up floor plans and expedite approvals from the Department of Buildings, she was also unlicensed, so her services came at a steep discount.

JOHN, CONSTRUCTION

One of Robert's younger brothers, who'd just finished his junior year at the College of William and Mary in Virginia. He was tireless and could lift ten times as much as anyone else on the crew. We paid him eighty dollars a day and all the beer and pizza he wanted.

STEVE, CONSTRUCTION

An out-of-work actor friend who was happy for any gig he could get, as long as he could practice his audition monologues while hammering.

FRANK, ELECTRICIAN

Robert ran into Frank at a party and offhandedly mentioned that we were looking for an electrician. Frank immediately volunteered. Not only was he a skilled electrician, but he also knew how to run a job site, keeping track of the comings and goings of various subcontractors. His head was like a blender full of Post-it notes, and somehow it all made sense to him.

Aaron wasn't the most experienced contractor on the block. In fact, when he showed up for the job interview, I thought he was at the wrong house—he looked so young! We tried to grill him with tough questions to make sure he was cut out for the job. Of course, we were as green as he was, so we were all making it up as we went along. "Have you ever done anything like this before?" I asked him. "Build a house?"

"Not really," he said, being honest. "I was an apprentice carpenter for a few years in Baltimore, and I worked on a few houses."

Had he ever been a general contractor? No, he hadn't. Had he ever done any framing? "Well," he said, "we framed a couple of houses last summer. My boss's woodwork is beautiful."

We were so new to this, we didn't recognize this as a potential red flag. Wood framing in New York is meaningless. Carpenters have been framing in metal in the city since at least the 1950s. But we were both like, "Hey, he knows about wood framing! That sounds like something!"

But what really sold us were his confidence and friendly demeanor. We took him to the second floor with all the same tiny rooms. Almost everybody else had grimaced at that point. Aaron looked around and nodded like he already had a plan worked out in his head. We told him right away, "We're on a tight budget. We can do $75 a square foot at the very most. Can you make that work?"

He just smiled, kept studying the rooms, and finally said, "Sure, that's doable." He didn't explain how. It was enough for us that he didn't seem rattled by any of it. He wasn't telling us all the ways it wasn't possible. He was just, like, "Sure, let's do this." "Yes, that's possible." "Yeah, definitely. We can try that!" We needed "yes" people like Aaron. We needed people in our midst who believed that despite all appearances, we could create something amazing.

Robert and I didn't even wait until we were alone to discuss it. Aaron barely said goodbye before we offered him the job. I think our exact words were, "Can you start on Monday?"

And now the real work could begin.

"

Don't be afraid to ask questions, and listen hard to the answers. People will teach you almost anything if you show some curiosity about their expertise. Being eager to learn goes a long way.

Our vision was to restore the place to its original 1830s glory, but without a nineteenth-century aesthetic. In other words, we weren't looking to do a historical preservation. We didn't want people to walk in and feel like they were back in the Victorian era. For one thing, that wasn't in our budget or skill set at all. What we wanted was the *feel* of the house to be restored. We wanted to transform this closed-off grid of tiny, dusty cubicles into large, open rooms, high ceilings, huge windows, and a grand parlor floor.

The first step was demo. While Marie and Cortney drafted up the plans together—it turned out Cortney was great at space layout and understanding architectural plans—we'd gut the place and get rid of everything we didn't want or need. Which was pretty much all of it *and* the kitchen sink. The only problem was, we didn't have permits yet.

I called Joe and asked what he thought. Should we wait for the paperwork? He said, "Of course you can start. You don't need a permit to clean." So we started cleaning, and a little more, until the required permits came through.

While I went to my finance job—my paycheck was the only thing keeping the lights on at that point—Aaron and Cortney got right to it, knocking down walls on every floor. Cortney became much more than an on-site manager. At twenty-three, she jumped in with both arms and a sledgehammer.

It was exhilarating! Aside from the demolition being a great tension release, I felt genuine gratification smashing down those walls. Once all the makeshift rooms were gone, creating wide-open spaces, I was on cloud nine. I could see more clearly what the house could become. All those walls had made it feel so cramped. Now you could see how much space was actually there. And once we took the boards off the windows—the place was technically condemned, don't forget—light flooded in and it was downright magical. That said, now that we could see the house in all its glory, we could also see the insane amount of dust and chunks of debris.

Gutting and rebuilding

Still, it was glorious.

We weren't able to salvage much except for a few significant pieces: the front door, the red staircase, and the fireplace mantel—though we didn't yet have enough cash to get the fireplace itself going. But we were in no hurry to get it fixed. We would get to it later, long after we finished restoring the house and moved in. This was a lesson we learned early on: you don't have to do everything at once.

And then there was that day you fell through the floor.

Oh, yes, that was a fun day. We'd gotten rid of most of the floors. We knew we couldn't afford to replace all the beams, but structurally we had to replace some. One day I was up on the third floor, stepping from beam to beam, and I must've lost my footing, because I tripped and fell two floors. It happened so fast, I didn't have time to panic. I caught myself on one of the beams. I was like an amateur gymnast. It was pretty spectacular. I don't know if I could've done it on purpose; it was like my survival instinct kicked in. I was about to go *splat* on the concrete floor, and it was either that or flail for the first piece of wood I could grab and cling to it like a spider monkey. In other words, there was never a dull moment!

All that rubble Aaron and Cortney were creating had to go somewhere. So we rented a container, big as a dump truck, and parked it outside. After the first day of demo, there was still plenty of room for more wreckage—a good thing, too, as it'd cost us several hundred dollars every time the container had to be emptied. The more we could jam in there, the better. With the intention to fill it to the brim the next day, we left it on the street, open to the elements, and went home for the night.

New York was about to teach us a harsh lesson in trust.

When we showed up the next morning, the container was filled to the brim with trash. The neighbors had used it as their own private dumpster. And they didn't just throw garbage bags in there—there were saggy mattresses, busted TVs, broken windows, floor lamps, boxes of old magazines, cracked dishes, greasy cookware, and at least one car tire. I couldn't believe it. I guess the "NO PUBLIC DUMPING" sign on the container wasn't enough to deter them. I admit it must have been hard to resist such an easy way to get rid of your junk on someone else's dime.

So we invested in a tarp, thick and heavy, that was too big a pain in the ass for the neighbors to move out of the way so they could shove more old dishware in there. It was our way of saying hello to the new neighbors. In New York, sometimes a jaunty middle finger is the same as a wave.

Ten days later, we had an empty shell of a house. The next step would be more complicated, but in many ways more exciting. Now that the tearing down was over, it was time to rebuild.

Finishing touches

2

EMBRACE THE CHAOS
West Nineteenth Street
Chelsea, New York

"I don't think you understand who you're dealing with, lady," John grumbled through the phone in his thick New Yawk accent.

I tried to stay calm, but I wasn't going to budge and I told him as much. "We're not paying you until you finish the job."

Truth be told, I was in no position to be telling a veteran New York cement guy how to do his job. He'd been pouring grout in Gotham since before I was born. But I'd lived on the island long enough to know that New Yorkers can smell fear.

"I want my damn money," he barked at me.

"Well then finish pouring our damn basement floor," I shouted back, matching his volume.

He rattled off a bunch of expletives—some really impressive cursing, if memory serves—before finally snarling, "This is not how things are done."

"Well, it's how *we* do things," I told him. "If I need to find another cement guy, let me know so I can stop wasting my time."

When all the permits had been filed and the plans drafted, we brought in subcontractors to do the structural work—building new walls and floors, setting up the electricity and plumbing, pouring the cement. We found most of them either by word of mouth or the yellow pages. (Remember the yellow pages?! Yes, I let my fingers do the walking.) No Google, no Nextdoor, no place to read reviews or hear other peoples' stories to help us make a decision. We had to just pluck a name out of the ether or the phone book, or meet them at parties we threw, and hope for the best.

When I first found our cement guy, it didn't occur to me to pause at his last name.

Gotti.

His last name was Gotti.

Oh...no.

Probably not the best approach, I told Cortney, to play hardball with an Italian with the last name Gotti who lives in New York and says things like "Don't you know who I am?" But Cortney is fearless and not easily intimidated, so I knew she wasn't going to back down. In the end, we paid him and the job got done. But we were a little shaky for a few weeks, looking over our shoulders, wondering if we'd end up in the bottom of a cement mixer "by accident."

Although each step of the process brought new issues and challenges, it was all worth it. The best part, the most fun, was looking for new ways to make our first house into something special, something uniquely its own. The blueprints only tell you where the walls and hallways go. They don't tell you how to give a house its distinct personality.

And that part's important—beautiful aesthetics—though there will always be imperfections. Thankfully, they sometimes turn out to be the best part. Cortney and I do our best to let go a little and not hold on too tight to the look of things being perfect. Your design should have character, for sure, and it will, inevitably, reflect something of *your* character back into the house.

But there *are* things that should be as close to perfect as possible: plumbing, for example. The electrics, too, the air and heating systems. And, for gosh sake, make sure you build the most perfect new roof!

Speaking of working with imperfection…during the renovation, as we got down to the bare walls, we discovered large, beautiful areas of exposed brick. We loved everything about it. It felt cozy and Old World—two things we wanted the house's personality to shine with. Unfortunately, the brick was on an exterior wall, so we couldn't leave it as is, since it had to be insulated. So we decided to save some of the bricks from the demo and hire bricklayers to build internal archways to separate the dining room from the kitchen. It was exciting to consider not having to completely ditch them. And, in the absence of an actual door, the archways would make the kitchen feel more like its own distinct space while still allowing the bright southern light coming through the back windows to filter through the rest of the main floor.

Because we didn't have enough bricks for the entire archway, we scavenged for old, weathered bricks at other job sites. We could've gone the easy way and found a bunch of store-bought bricks that looked fresh out of the kiln, but we wanted something that felt more authentic, like it belonged in the house and wasn't slapped on to modernize it. I think of new materials in old houses like the lip fillers of architecture. One of my priorities as a designer with this kind of project—an aging building with good bones and unique features—is to not hide the home's age. It doesn't need to look younger and hotter. Let it show off its wrinkles!

So, anywhere they were giving away bricks or where we were allowed to dig around in the rubble, we were there, digging around, enjoying the treasure hunt. I loved watching the bricklayers build the archway. It was beautiful, the artistry involved. A reminder that okay, some things we can do ourselves, and some things we need to leave to the pros.

That said, after watching the bricklayers, we thought maybe we had the technique down. So we tried laying bathroom tiles on our own, an attempt that didn't last long. It did not bring out our better sides. Maybe we're not as handy as we'd like to be, but you can't be too full of hubris, doing this work. You learn when to cut corners and do something yourself because you can probably figure it out, and when to find skilled workers and stand aside. Sometimes you learn this the hard way!

Because the majority of our budget went into the structural work, we had almost no money left for furnishings. So we set our sights on flea markets and antique stores. We bought old chairs and couches and had them reupholstered; we found funky iron beds and painted them; we stained and painted furniture; we cut mirrors for tabletops; we found fantastic vintage hardware for doorknobs and light fixtures. We borrowed a lot of our concepts from ABC Carpet & Home, our favorite store at the time. We loved their paint schemes, lighting, fabrics, and decoration ideas—we just couldn't afford them. So we tried to reproduce them with whatever we could find elsewhere. We've always loved old things, pieces of furniture that are a little lived in and have a story and a life; they bring a sense of history and story into a house. The more weathered and beaten up, the better.

During one of our many flea market trips, long before we found the Chelsea house, we'd picked up a huge white column. We had no idea why—pure instinct. We kept it in our tiny apartment, where it looked ridiculous, but we loved it and knew we'd find a space for it someday. It ended up being one of the first pieces we installed in the new home. It was as if we'd been fostering it until we found the home it was meant for. It belonged there, looking regal and showing off the height of our ceilings.

"

You learn when to cut corners and do something yourself because you can probably figure it out, and when to find skilled workers and stand aside. Sometimes you learn this the hard way!

Address plate on West Nineteenth Street

We learned through so many furniture hunts that it was way more fun—and successful—when we let go of rigid ideas about what we wanted. We never went looking for antiques or secondhand furniture with a checklist: "We need this, this, this, and this." We waited until we stumbled upon something and realized, "Yes! That's the piece we've been looking for and never knew until now!" The anticipation of what we might find, how we would use it, where we would put it made it an adventure. When we salvaged old library shelves from Dartmouth College, we didn't know they'd end up in our bedroom someday. We picked up a barber's chair just because it looked cool, not realizing that it'd be a perfect fit for our living room. We allowed ourselves to be surprised.

Some of our decorating ideas didn't go over so well with the neighbors. New Yorkers have a lot of opinions, and they're not afraid to share them. One morning I was outside planting flowers in the flower boxes when someone decided to stop and give me their two cents—though it was more like twenty-five—about the painted yellow exterior of the house. If memory serves, the woman told me it was "too sunny" and "too yellow." What were we thinking painting our house such a ridiculous color? "Well, it's nice to meet you, too!" is what I wanted to say. But my Southern roots kicked in and I just smiled and said, "Thank you so much. I'll take that into consideration."

Sometimes the neighbors could be helpful, like when a pair of local hippie guys—or, as they introduced themselves, "academic archaeologists"—knocked on our front door and asked if they could dig up the privy in our backyard. We had no clue what a privy was. Turns out it's an old outdoor bathroom set back from the main house, common in Manhattan until the mid-nineteenth century (when indoor plumbing became a thing) and now considered to have archaeological value. In addition to its primary purpose, privies were used by residents as trash receptacles—and when the privy wasn't needed anymore, as a place to get rid of old crockery, glass bottles, and other household items that no longer had any use. Some of the townhouses in our neighborhood were owned by wealthy sea captains, so some privies of these once-waterfront homes have turned out bottles and other objects from historic ships that came and went from the Chelsea piers.

The archaeologists next door said they'd give us anything of value they found. So for a couple of weeks, while we were building and decorating, there were two guys doing a dig in our backyard where the bathroom used to be. "Found any dead bodies yet?" one plumber yelled out the window. They pulled out tons of stuff: gorgeous purple-glass milk bottles, chipped porcelain dishes and transferware plate fragments, a child's clay marble, a glass oil lamp, a clay pipe and stem, a small medicine bottle, a chocolate-glazed shard from a cooking crock, and what looked like a magical brass key, which they proposed might be the original key to the house.

Sometimes the neighbors even contributed decor. One day while I was walking to work, I noticed a beautiful stained glass church window in someone's backyard. It was just leaning up against a wall, like they'd been planning to do something with it and then forgot. I wanted it so badly. I mentioned it to Robert, and he reminded me that somebody's backyard is not a store. "It's not for sale," he said. "Forget about it!"

But I couldn't let it go. "It's just sitting there! Nobody is using it!" I could barely stand it. So one afternoon finally I walked over and knocked. I explained that I'd been admiring the stained glass window in their backyard and asked if they'd consider selling it. Turns out they didn't even know it was back there, and just gave it to me! Sometimes all you have to do is ask.

On top of all the insanity of renovating a home in New York on a shoe-string budget, we were multitasking with another huge project that felt like it could spiral out of control at any moment: our upcoming wedding in Cortney's home state. It was to be a lively four-day extravaganza in Upatoi with five hundred guests, a gospel choir, several bands, and a catered sit-down dinner. I was still working full-time in finance while Cortney, when not at the job site, was flying down South to plan our nuptials. Were we nuts to do both the wedding and the house in the same year? Yes, we were. At the time, though, we just kept following Cortney's philosophy for rehabbing our home, applying it to everything: "What needs to get done *today*?"

To be fair, though, we knew by now that we thrived on chaos. The more balls we had in the air, the better we performed and the more we got done. Ideas for the wedding and the house fed into and off of each other.

That's so true. One afternoon when I was working in the house, I uncovered ancient floral wallpaper, and while I could take or leave the wallpaper itself, I fell in love with its color palette and decided to use it for our wedding. When we picked burlap tablecloths to go underneath the white lace tablecloths that draped to the floor, it inspired oversize burlap pillows for the house. When you're in that creative space, it comes out in everything you do.

The wedding, just like the house rehab, was not without its missteps—no true disasters, but not everything went exactly according to plan, either. The cake caught on fire when my drunk and crazy cousin from Allentown, Pennsylvania, had an after-party in the small storage area where our cake happened to be; we forgot to pick up the priest at the airport (and he flew back home rather than wait); Cortney's dress got so beat up and covered in grass stains from dancing so hard that she looked like she'd been playing football; and to round out the evening, someone complained about the too-loud music so the cops showed up as our final wedding guests.

Needless to say, it was one of the best nights of our lives.

In a weird way, the wedding was also a boot camp for the kinds of challenges we'd face as home designers—not just with the Chelsea house, but in every project we'd eventually take on. We had two choices: we could drown in a tsunami of worry and planning, trying to control everything and ultimately having little control over much of anything, grinding our teeth every time things didn't go exactly according to plan, or we could lean into the chaos, enjoy the maelstrom, and learn to be flexible.

I generally came home to the job site every day during my lunch break. And then I'd be back every evening at five o'clock, the moment the markets closed. I had an end-of-the-day routine where I'd deal with the subcontractors, pay the bills, coordinate projects for the next day, and clean for an hour or so. Cleaning is a huge stress reliever for me. It's psychic comfort to sweep up, clean windows, carry trash out. And then I'd just sit by myself on those Hong Kong–red stairs and think about how different this was from everything else I did all day. The changes happening to the house were tangible. I could touch them, I could see them. I could see our future taking shape right in front of me. Nothing happening at my job on Wall Street was tangible. It was just numbers; I wasn't building toward something. But this—this was real. This was *ours*.

Even when things were at their craziest and it looked like everything could fall apart, we tried to find moments to just sit together and consciously appreciate everything. "This is all happening right here in this moment, and we're not getting this moment again. Let's pause."

Sometimes when it would get overwhelming, feel like too much, we'd just sit on the floor—the unfinished, dirty hardwood floor—and remind each other, "If we can get through this, just get to the other side, then we'll *own a building in New York City*. We'll have a piece of this city's history." It's almost like the old wood beneath us was saying: "Just finish. Get it done. Stop worrying."

It's so much about enjoying the process, not getting too swept up in the minutiae. "Stop worrying about the tile; the tile's being delivered. Let's just be present."

Even when things were at
their craziest and it looked
like everything could
fall apart, we tried to find
moments to just sit together
and consciously appreciate
everything. 'This is all
happening right here in
this moment, and we're not
getting this moment again.
Let's pause.'

By fall 1996, less than a year after we first toured the house with Joe, we were finished. The walls were sealed, the floors stained and polished, the utility lines hooked up, the light fixtures turned on. The toilets all flushed. We'd passed all the inspections and received our certificate of occupancy, the official document from New York's Department of Buildings stating that a house is safe to live in. It was the document we needed to finally get a bank loan and pay Joe the rest of the money we owed him.

Eventually he would come by to see it finished. He'd visited a few times during construction, looking impressed and slightly envious, humble and humbled. He connected us with a few subcontractors along the way, too. He even took us out to lunch to mark the occasion of the house's finish, regaling us with his own New York stories, yelling for the waiter, showing us maybe that he was a *real* New Yorker, unlike us. We didn't mind. He was our linchpin, had done us a true favor from which everything else that came after sprang.

It was surreal to realize we were officially homeowners now, and specifically owners of a townhouse. I grew up loving old things—comic books, baseball cards, autographs. When my family lived in Alexandria, I'd tag along to estate sales with my mom—an antique dealer—and my dad. There's a historic area right along the Potomac River called Old Town that has all of these amazing eighteenth-century townhouses. We would go there on the weekends just to walk the streets and look at the homes, which seemed so cozy and inviting. My mom always had a dream that one day, somebody in the family would own a townhouse in Old Town. It seemed like such an unrealistic fantasy at the time. Who could afford something like that? Certainly not any of us. But it planted the seed in my head.

And now, here I was. Here *we* were, my new wife and I, still technically young adults, with our own townhouse that we'd brought back to life. It was almost ready for move-in, and the timing couldn't have been more perfect. Thanksgiving was around the corner and Cortney was pregnant.

Did we not mention that yet? During most of the renovation, I was pregnant with our first child, Wolfgang. We decided to host my entire family for the holiday, inviting them up from Georgia to stay in our new Chelsea digs. There was just one small problem: the gas hadn't been turned on yet, so we had no hot water and couldn't cook a turkey. It was 20 degrees outside, which was not exactly an ideal temperature for hosting guests, especially Southerners. The gas company said it could be weeks before they'd be able to schedule us. But then I came up with a plan.

I saw a few gas line workers down the street, working in the freezing cold. So I immediately ran to the bakery, bought a huge box of cookies and a half dozen hot chocolates, and took it all over to them. I made sure to waddle so they could tell I was in a family way. Then I asked, in my sweetest pregnant-mama voice, "Is there any way you kind gentlemen could help us out of a jam?"

We had heat that afternoon. It was a holiday miracle.

My family arrived two days later to a warm house with all the lights on. Two vehicles with Georgia and Alabama license plates, overstuffed like clown cars with family—my mom and dad, sister and brother, brother-in-law, a few aunts and uncles, and cousins—and all their luggage pulled up to our curb, ready to "baptize" the new house. The house was done, but not "done-done." It was still very much a work in progress. We gave them a tour, and they immediately wanted to pitch in.

My Aunt Marsha had packed a sewing machine. She studied the curtains in our living room and immediately decided they needed proper hems.

"Where'd you get those flimsy things?" she asked.

I told her money was tight and we had had to cut some corners: we'd doubled up two sets of short curtains so they'd look like one long panel. Aunt Marsha wasn't having it. She was determined to fix those curtains straightaway, but I told her we could probably wait until *after* Thanksgiving.

The place was still pretty bare, and we didn't even have a proper dining room table yet. So we threw a tablecloth on a "gang box," a huge toolbox common on construction sites, and used that as a makeshift buffet. It made Thanksgiving feel like a picnic. But we didn't need a lot of flash. We showed them what was probably our favorite part of the house: the roof and its unobstructed view of the Empire State Building. It was pretty amazing to lounge in a chair, reading a book, then look up and see one of the world's most iconic skyscrapers.

Next stop on the tour was the unfurnished third floor. There were two large bedrooms separated by a loft space in the middle. Each bedroom had an air mattress and not much else. The closets didn't even have rods or shelves yet. But my parents made sure the house didn't look empty for long. They went out to their cars and brought in all these beautiful Georgia plants and a wisteria tree. We never could've afforded any of it in New York (good luck finding a wisteria tree on discount!).

Then we showed them the baby's room, which predictably elicited the most excitement from my mother and aunts. We'd started decorating it, but there was only so much we could spend with all the renovation costs. We'd found an antique crib, an old dresser that we turned into a changing table, and a vintage trunk for toys. The only thing missing, at least according to Aunt Marsha, was a rocking chair. "How are you gonna rock your child to sleep without a rocking chair?" she asked, like it was something we should've prioritized ahead of plumbing and insulation. When I agreed that we'd look into getting one as soon as we had a few extra dollars, she turned and left, her feet pitter-pattering down the stairs.

Robert and I looked at each other, both of us wondering, "Is she leaving?"

She was back a few minutes later—not with a rocker but with a tiny chest of drawers, the very same chest of drawers from my house growing up in Georgia where we kept all the baby clothes from my sisters and me. It had been passed on to Marsha's daughters, and now she was passing it on to me. "It's yours now, Cortney," she told me. "Maybe this time, it'll get used for a boy."

We filled that house with life for Thanksgiving, baptized it with laughter and stories, making it into the home where Robert and I could start our family. In the background, our boom box (our very high-end sound system at the time) warmed the house with holiday music, a notable change from the months on end when "shock jock" Howard Stern's loud voice echoed through the rooms while the team worked away. I could not have asked for a better holiday or better company. There was just one question nagging at us, which my mom brought up somewhere in the middle of dinner: "The house is beautiful," she said. "You did such an amazing job. But I'm curious, how are you going to pay for it?"

We didn't have an answer. We'd spent everything we had on the renovation, and there was still so much left to do. My job was paying the bills, but not enough to keep up with our mortgage. And we still had expenses beyond that. The house had running water, electricity, and four sturdy walls, but there was a lot more work to be done, like drapes for the street-facing windows on the first floor. It wasn't until we moved in and started living there that we realized our life was like a big Macy's window display.

We had to find another source of income, and that meant roommates. Well, not roommates exactly. Tenants. But we didn't want strangers living with us, so we reached out to friends—the twentysomething actors and restaurant workers we socialized with and trusted implicitly—and invited them to rent rooms. Even in mid-1990s New York, when finding affordable housing wasn't yet the crisis it would become, it was still a good deal. Besides, most rental situations don't come with the occasional home-cooked meal. Within just a few weeks, three people had taken us up on our offer. Steve, an aspiring Broadway actor who had worked on the construction crew, took one of the many bedrooms, and my sister Jacqueline and her boyfriend moved into the "garden" (aka basement) apartment.

Our generous friends kept volunteering to help us decorate, maybe motivated by the fact that we were living a life they could aspire to. As we've mentioned, not many people in their twenties were buying homes in the city then, or even now. You rent an apartment, and you stay there until you're ready to buy a home somewhere outside the city limits. But we jumped ahead and got the home when most people our age—including us—weren't 100 percent sure where our next meal was coming from. Here we were in this big, old building, able to do anything we wanted to it. If we wanted to repaint, knock down a wall, or tear out a fireplace and rebuild it, we didn't need anybody's permission but our own.

We spent afternoons with our eager friends, exploring flea markets and thrift stores across the city, convincing them that it was great fun to dig through the dusty artifacts of some store that looked like a dump truck had pulled up to the front and unloaded. It was a fine way to spend a Saturday afternoon. But as enthusiastic as our friends were, they weren't always up for what we had in mind. We'd all be out partying till dawn—as you do when you're young—and then Cortney and I would be up bright and early the next morning, knocking on doors.

"Anybody want to take a drive out to Queens to check out an estate sale?" They'd look at us with bloodshot eyes and wave us off their doorstep.

By the time they were stumbling out for brunch, we'd be half a world away, shoving old wall sconces into our trunk.

One of our favorite antiquing haunts back then, and still, is Olde Good Things, a chain with locations across New York, Pennsylvania, and Los Angeles. The true finds can usually be found at their Scranton location, a two-hour drive northwest of the city. The Olde Good Things warehouse is two hundred thousand square feet of ever-changing inventory with mysteries in every corner, but it's not always open to the public. We'd spend entire weekends digging through old porcelain sinks, stained glass windows, brass doorknobs.

Because Scranton was once an industrial hub—iron and coal were big business there in the mid-nineteenth century—it's a one-stop shop for any and all manner of antique iron and metalwork. If you're a vigilant New Yorker with a tank full of gas and a Saturday to kill, go! You might head home with a wrought iron railing or cast-iron bathtub for a steal.*

I once made the mistake of bringing a friend with me on one of my Scranton trips. I told her, "I'm looking for old doors. Want to come hunting with me?" Which sounds like a fun adventure, right? Couple of girls window-shopping for antiques, then maybe getting lunch. So we got in the car for the two-hour trip out to basically the middle of nowhere. Scranton is great, but it's not exactly a tourist hot spot. No charming gourmet country stores. No hipster coffee shops or trendy bakeries. I took my friend to a warehouse—an actual warehouse, not a cute little emporium with the scent of potpourri in the air—and got to work, hoping to find a gem of an interior door in their collection of hundreds, while my friend sat to the side. The more doors I pawed through, the more upset she got. I watched as it slowly dawned on her that this was it, our big adventure: literally looking for old doors in Scranton. No alternative agenda. No day drinking disguised as work. I was looking for a door and was not leaving until I found the perfect one. She remarked, huffily, "Remind me not to join you next time."

In May 1997, six months after we moved in, we came home from the hospital with our first son, Wolfgang. As we pulled up to the house, Wolfie in my arms, I looked out from the taxi window and saw sixty blue balloons tied to our front stoop. I was hormonal and

---

*This is not a paid endorsement, but the authors are happy to accept donations and gift certificates from Olde Good Things, should they be so inclined.

emotional already, but there was something about that moment, arriving at the home that Robert and I had made, that seemed so improbable. We'd somehow pulled it off, and now our son! It just made me sob. Such a significant moment. I carried the baby up the stairs and through the old blue double doors, tears streaming down my face, Robert at our side. Inside were our roommates—the friends who'd become like family—waiting to meet the newest member of the tribe. Some of them had never held a baby before. It's possible that even I hadn't until that day. It was a beautiful moment, and I'm forever glad we experienced it there, in that house we'd made. It felt like home. But was it our forever home?

That was the big question. It felt like it could be. We didn't know yet that what we'd accomplished with this house was just the beginning. We didn't know that Robert would quit Wall Street. That over and over we'd buy old buildings that nobody believed in and transform them into homes, into something truly special, marked by our unique touch, then move on to the next one. We didn't know yet that we'd do this for the rest of our lives. I came to New York City because I had big dreams and knew that the city was going to play a pivotal role in those dreams, even though I had no idea how. Robert and I knew that more kids were in our future—or we certainly hoped so—and we wanted our life to keep expanding and opening up. We just weren't sure how it was all going to happen.

And then someone came knocking.

The guy at our door told us he had a client who wanted to rent the place. Not just a bedroom or two—the *whole* place. We were like, "Thanks, but no, it's not for rent." It had never crossed our minds that this was something we would do. We didn't even have a for-rent sign outside.

Then the broker told us who he was there representing, who his client was: Grammy-winning singer-songwriter Suzanne Vega, famous for hit songs like "Tom's Diner" and "Luka." He explained that Suzanne

A house of our own, for a minute

had recently been strolling down West Nineteenth Street and noticed our yellow townhouse. It stood out, as the neighborhood was still pretty gray and coldly urban—a pre-gentrified look that would change in the coming years—and so the singer was charmed and instantly knew this was where she wanted to live with her two-year-old daughter, Ruby. So she'd sent the broker over with an offer.

And it was quite an offer. She was proposing to rent the place for a figure that after some quick math turned out to be four times our monthly mortgage payment. *Four times!* We were floored. It was a ridiculous amount of money. With a bit more math, we realized that if we took her up on her offer, we wouldn't just cover our expenses; we'd be *ahead*. It was unthinkable at the time, especially given that we hadn't designed the home with anybody but ourselves in mind. We didn't make a single choice thinking, "Is this going to attract high-end buyers?" Not to mention a renter for the whole house. We were just thinking about our own aesthetics, what made *us* happy. It was crazy to think we'd created something that could have outside appeal, *profitable* appeal.

Then came the hard part. We had to ask our friends to move out. They absolutely understood, of course, that we couldn't say no to that kind of money. Their rent had helped us quite a bit, but we were still struggling to make ends meet. The good news was that Suzanne only wanted the top three floors. We were free to stay in the garden apartment, which had its own private entrance, so we wouldn't even run into each other. Not that that was a problem, because we became fast friends with Suzanne and her daughter. We'd all hang out on the front stoop and talk, and she'd play songs—for all of us, but mostly for Wolfgang and Ruby. She even wrote a beautiful song for Wolfie's christening.

It was a great arrangement, but we knew it couldn't last forever. It was just the three of us for now—Robert, Wolfie, and me—but we knew our family would grow. And unbeknownst to us, I was already

pregnant again—with twins! The garden apartment wouldn't, when the time came, offer space enough to hold us all.

So, what to do with that positive cash flow? We'd never had positive cash flow before. We could buy something move-in ready and not put ourselves through all that struggle again. Or we could jump on our Vespa and drive around the city to see what else was out there. I don't think Robert and I ever discussed it explicitly, but in my head, and I knew in his as well, we didn't want our next home to be something with built-in personality. We didn't want the most popular kid on the block, the house with the prettiest shutters or the most welcoming exterior—the one everyone with cash to burn would be elbowing one another to get to first. We wanted the opposite of that. In fact, we wanted something *worse* than the Chelsea townhouse when we first found it.

We wanted a bigger, more absurd challenge. Nothing less than the wreck of the century.

Transforming a corner in SoHo

3

WRECK OF THE CENTURY
22 & 24 Thompson Street
SoHo, New York

One of my favorite restaurants in New York, maybe on the planet, is Felix, a classic French bistro that's been on the corner of West Broadway and Grand Street in SoHo for thirty years. Its corner location gives it great energy, along with the team behind the restaurant: the French owner, Alain Denneulin; his wife, Angela, who hails from Brazil; and their longtime Filipina host, Thea. My mom said once that Felix was more French than any restaurant she'd ever been to in France: "More Paris than Paris." She's right! And there's no more glorious way to spend a summer afternoon than sitting at a table near Felix's French double doors that open onto the sidewalk, people watching while sipping wine and munching on tuna tartare and steak frites.

At some point in 1998 or thereabouts, while talking with Alain—we're still friends to this day—I mentioned that Cortney and I were looking for our next project.

"Have you checked out the place around the corner?" he asked.

"Around the corner where?"

"On Thompson," he said, pointing down the street. "It's right around the block."

Thompson? I'd been coming to this corner for years and didn't even consider that ugly commercial building as a possible home for our family, since we had only been looking at townhouses. Once we discovered that the nondescript building could be rezoned for residential, it opened a whole new world of possibilities. That's how easy it is to miss the really great finds, especially in New York. You miss the treasures if you're not constantly exploring with an open mind.

"Keep my tab open," I said, jumping out of my seat. "I'll be right back."

"It's an eyesore," Alain yelled as I disappeared down the street. He didn't know that a comment like that wasn't exactly discouraging.

But he wasn't kidding. The property for sale wasn't just any old falling-apart building. It was a condemned commercial space (a former grocery store) with zero charm. Utterly neglected.

On paper, it got less ugly. It was a three-story building on a corner piece of property. And though we had little experience, we knew, thanks to conversations with and guidance from those who'd gone before us, that if you have the means and opportunity to buy *anything* on a corner—a commercial, retail, or residential building—snatch it up! The possibilities are huge. You have more options for light, for windows and entrances—just more potential all around.

The asking price for this sad property? A little over half a million. Even though its address wasn't in the "nice" part of SoHo, and it was zoned for commercial use, not residential, this still wasn't a bad asking price. The owner even agreed to throw in the dirty parking lot next door, which according to him was too small to build anything on. The sliver of space was just that, a sliver, and full of trash.

There were things to consider, though—namely, the rezoning of the building from commercial to residential. This would involve filing a lot of paperwork with the city and getting a lot of approvals from not just city officials but also the neighbors. If you've never experienced

Cortney in the vacant lot at 24 Thompson Street

trying to get a building response, imagine trying to get your driver's license renewed, but in addition to visiting your local DMV, you've also got to show up for several public hearings in which everyone you might potentially drive to or near gets to vote on whether you should be allowed behind the wheel. It's a lengthy, paperwork-laden review process with the local community board, the borough president, and the city planning commission.

I immediately called Cortney to come take a look, and she thought the same thing I did.

Let's take it!

It wasn't just about the building's potential and everything we could do with it. We were buying this eyesore for the *neighborhood* as well.

SoHo—for you non–New Yorkers, that's shorthand for South of Houston Street in Lower Manhattan—was a manufacturing hub before it became an oasis for struggling artists looking for loft spaces they could inhabit for next to nothing. Many even squatted in vacant buildings and lived rent free. As a longtime resident once told the *New York Times*, "No one but artists wanted to live here. You had to hide from building inspectors and paper over the windows so they couldn't see the lights on at night."

This was not an area in the city where potential buyers asked, "How are the schools? What are the test scores like?" There were no schools to speak of, much less garbage pickup or grocery stores. But if you pay attention, if you listen to what the locals are discussing (or arguing about) and read about the businesses plotting to move in down the street, you can get a pretty decent idea of where a neighborhood might be heading versus where it's been.

People talk about wishing they could invent a time machine to go back and invest in Apple stock before anyone knew what Apple would become. But imagine going back to the late 1990s, on the cusp of SoHo's transformation from an empty warehouse district with historic but abandoned cast-iron factory buildings to a retail and residential destination. When we arrived, it was still an enclave for artists and bohemians, who, by and large (and understandably), wanted to keep it like they'd found it. But imagine being there at the start of the new SoHo and seeing what it could become? (We were!) Just as a for-instance, in this reawakened version, an artist who wanted to raise a family, send their kids to good schools, and potentially have more opportunities to prosper with a higher-earning clientele could do so while still living in the middle of one of the coolest neighborhoods in New York. The potential and possibilities might take time to manifest, but they were inevitable.

When friends and family learned what we were planning, they yet again tried to talk us out of it. Nobody—or at least nobody who truly cares—will tell you to jump off the highest bridge or mountain. You have to make that choice yourself. Once we made the offer on the house, my parents came to visit, and we took them to see it. They sat across the street on a bench, dumbfounded, staring at this crumbling building that seemed to have nothing to offer but urban blight. They weren't even able to put on a brave face. They sincerely thought we were going to lose everything. They loved us and believed in us, but they also thought we were in over our heads. And they might've been right. But we were stubborn.

Sometimes you have to close your eyes and jump.

It helps that Robert and I both believed together. Having a partner who's as crazy as you are is vital, or it has been for us. You can take turns being blindly optimistic. On the days that I was scared, Robert wasn't. And on the days he was scared, I wasn't. Every day, though, we weren't focusing on the abandoned factories and the graffiti and the lack of thriving businesses. We knew there were exciting things on the horizon. Like the SoHo Grand, a 370-room hotel that was being built right around the corner from the Thompson Street building. It was the first hotel in SoHo in at least a century. The locals weren't crazy about it. They were certain that it'd attract tour buses and overflow the sewers, but like it or not, the hotel was coming. And that meant a cultural shift for the entire neighborhood.

Robert and I weren't fazed by the bar culture that dominated much of the area. We also didn't mind that our new building was directly across the street from Naked Lunch at 17 Thompson, an infamous watering hole named after the William S. Burroughs novel (although it had nothing, not an awning or even a cocktail napkin, with that name on it—you either knew what it was called or you didn't), or Café Noir at 32 Grand Street, a Spanish tapas restaurant that never seemed to close. Café Noir would become an important spot for us, a hub of sorts for newfound friends and community in the neighborhood. It wasn't only bars, of course. Two streets over was the Performing Garage, home of the renowned Wooster Group theater company, cofounded by new and experimental talent, including Spalding Gray and Willem Dafoe.

Naked Lunch was owned by the Faheys, a fun, hardworking restaurant family. The patriarch, Pat, was up working as early as six o'clock in the morning, cleaning the bar and the street. Soon enough we formed a friendship, as at that hour I was usually up early shooting hoops with a very young Wolfgang in Thompson Street Park. Pat reminded me of my grandmother, who was from the same Queens neighborhood he was. Eventually he started coming to the park regularly to watch Wolfgang shoot hoops. A few years later, his grandson ended up on Wolfgang's tackle football team. New York City is truly a village, and SoHo was our community.

When we finally moved in, I remember feeding my children in the middle of the night, and I'd look out the window and there'd be a mob of people outside, dancing and singing. Someone separating from the revelers to cross the street and pee on our building wasn't unheard of. But it never bothered me. We were right in the middle of it, you know? Robert and I would have date night at Café Noir across the street and look over and see our children in the window. If you're going to choose to live where it's happening, then *live* where it's happening.

I loved Café Noir. It's gone now, but it was the kind of place only the locals seemed to know about. It wasn't famous-famous, even though it was featured in a few films. There's a famous sex scene in the Richard Gere movie *Unfaithful* that they shot in Café Noir's bathroom. Diane Lane, who plays a frustrated suburban housewife, has a steamy affair with Olivier Martinez, and they end up in the bathroom, and, well…

I myself never spent much time in the bathroom at Café Noir, but from the moment we started construction on Thompson, I was over there every chance I got. I didn't have a cell phone back then, but I did have a cordless phone, and the signal reached across the street. So I could wander over and have a drink and keep talking on the phone. Cortney could walk over with the baby and hand him to me while I was in the middle of a conversation. The whole block felt like an extension of our home. In my book, that feeling is every bit as important as square footage or the size of your backyard. It's true what they say, that New Yorkers mostly stay and live within a nine-block radius. For the most part, you don't have to go much farther than that for everything you need.

In our new neighborhood, there was a lot of exhilarating stuff happening almost all the time. One morning, for example, there was a photo shoot underway in front of Café Noir with the Beastie Boys! Cortney freaked! She was fifteen years old when she first saw them, in Columbus, Georgia. Her friends were going to see Hank Williams Jr., but not her. She'd discovered a passion for music, music videos, and pop culture by steeping herself in MTV (which was only six years old then!) and was not going to miss seeing one of her favorite bands. And it was a show that went down in Columbus history. The band nearly got themselves arrested, partly just for being the Beastie Boys but also, and maybe mostly, for the twenty-foot-tall inflatable penis that rose from the stage during the performance. Teenaged Cortney never forgot that! Now, twelve years later, here the band was, just outside our front door.

Later that same day, there was a fashion shoot in the same spot, and before I knew it I found myself in conversation with a few of the models during a break. These were supermodels, three of the most famous in the world at the time—Bridget Hall being one of them. The Beastie Boys in the morning and a *Vogue* photo shoot in the afternoon. Soho was definitely an exciting place to be, and we felt like we were part of the excitement. We had arrived!

It obviously isn't going to be that dramatic for everyone. But it *is* about looking for a mix of things. When you're considering buying a building, no matter where, it's important to look around and ask yourself: What do I like about the neighborhood that *already* exists? Then talk to people who live there—business owners, possible future neighbors. What's coming? What's going? When it comes down to it, all you need is one good coffee shop and one great grocery store.

You really have to approach it like a surfer looking for a wave. You don't wait for something huge, something obvious, to attract you to a property and its neighborhood. You're never going to get your board on top of that. It'll be too late. But if you study the water for ripples, you can steady yourself before the wave starts to grow, and then be part of it as it turns into something awesome. You have to get good at anticipating. It's not what it *is*, it's what it's *becoming*.

When we agreed to buy the building, there was a small part of us that felt—well, not cocky exactly, but definitely confident. The Chelsea townhouse had been a challenge, to put it lightly. Despite the big learning curves, though, we'd come out on the other side mostly unscathed. It wasn't easy, but it'd given us both a feeling of, "Hey, if that's as bad as it gets, we can do it again. Bring on the next house!"

Spoiler alert: that wasn't as bad as it gets.

The moment we put a bid on the property, we were already up against some very different obstacles than we'd faced before. The seller told us, "There's a small hiccup I should probably mention up front. Three different people think they own the place."

And I was like, "Wait, they *think* they do, or they do?" They were all suing each other, and it had the potential to get really ugly. We could either jump into the fray or sit this one out and wait for somebody to emerge when the dust settled. We opted for the latter. We were willing to walk away, and the only way we would close was if we could own it without strings attached.

At this point in our careers, we had two ironclad policies about investing in real estate. One, never buy a building with someone living in it. We always try to stay on the side of goodwill, and you don't want to be going through the process of evicting tenants on top of everything else involved with rehabbing a property. And two, never buy a building that's embroiled in a lawsuit. You're going to have enough to worry about once you actually own the building outright, and you don't need a bunch of people squabbling with you over the fine print on the deed. (There's actually a third that we'll go into a little later, which is the following: absolutely never buy a landmark building. It's a policy we've come to honestly and with the proverbial scars to prove it. Stay tuned!)

We needed a handful of zoning issues ironed out, too. So we helped the process along by negotiating with and buying out the owners of nearby buildings in order to settle the disputes so that before we began construction, we were the rightful owners.

Finally the building was ours, and we were ready to get going. But wait—there's more! We hit one more unfortunate snag before we could get things rolling in the right direction: a troubled and dishonest contractor. He seemed to know his stuff and was offering his services at a tantalizingly low price, which should have been the first warning sign, but we missed it. At the Chelsea house, we'd had Aaron, whom we loved and who saw us through to the end. But he'd decided to stick to finer carpentry rather than oversee large projects, and he moved to the New Jersey suburbs to start his own family. Subcontractors can be gruff sometimes and not always easy to manage. So we needed a new general contractor to supervise the ins and outs of the renovation.

At Thompson Street, we were already working with a tight budget—our financial windfall from Suzanne Vega's rent only went so far, especially after plunking down everything on this new property—and this guy was throwing out numbers that made our shoulders loosen. We thought the universe was cutting us a break, sending us a miracle. Not so much. It turned bad pretty quickly. Among other things, he'd show up to work intoxicated or not show up at all, and when we tried to fire him, he basically refused to be fired. He'd come back to work and refuse to leave. It only got worse from there. The details aren't as important as the fact that we could have avoided so much grief had we done our homework on this man. We'd had such great luck with our team in the past that we simply weren't on the lookout for problem people. It was a real lesson in how one small mistake can haunt you for months, even years.

The big takeaway (do we have to pick just one?) was that it's much easier to hire someone than it is to fire them. And it's better to cut your losses sooner rather than later. It can be pretty tough to accept the loss, but better to take it than risk the repercussions for your business, your new home to be, and your peace of mind.

As we had with the Chelsea townhouse, we made big structural changes to the SoHo property. There's something Cortney always says that I've taken as gospel: "You can bring charm to any four walls." In addition to the gut renovation, we added four "Juliet" balconies, replaced the brick facade with stucco, and installed new HVAC and plumbing. But the changes that really made the space were the ones that reflected our own aesthetic.

At nights, back at our garden apartment in Chelsea, we'd flip through magazines—because blogs were not yet a thing, we got most of our ideas from magazines—and cut out photos of any architecture or design that inspired us, taping images to the wall. We'd find old copies of *Architectural Digest* and dig through them like we were searching for clues. Anything we stumbled upon could be an inspiration. In today's design parlance, we were, instinctively, making a mood board to get our creativity and imaginations going.

Even though I was pregnant with twins, I was out there almost every day, looking for new pieces. I couldn't help myself. I loved digging through attics in old farmhouses or climbing fifty feet up some scaffolding to get a closer look at the facade on an old building. This wasn't out of character for me. I'm part redneck (pardon the political incorrectness, but it's just true). I was a wild child growing up in the South, definitely not your typical girl. I loved driving go-carts and riding motorcycles but also redecorated my room every year or

The big takeaway (do we have to pick just one?) was that it's much easier to hire someone than it is to fire them. And it's better to cut your losses sooner rather than later. It can be pretty tough to accept the loss, but better to take it than risk the repercussions for your business, your new home to be, and your peace of mind.

two. I once bought a waterbed in Atlanta with money I'd saved, the first and maybe only waterbed that existed in my small Southern town. Going on these field trips—lifting things, getting my hands into stockpiles—was second nature.

It didn't take long for Robert and me to become regulars at every antique store in the city. They knew us so well, they'd phone us with scoops. We'd get a call in the middle of the night from a dealer: "They're tearing down a chapel on 110th Street and turning it into condos. You want first dibs on the tile?" And the next morning, before most of the city had woken up, I'd be over there, pulling up tile and hauling it into a cab.

Some of our finds—like an old monastery gate we found at Olde Good Things—would need to be altered as we learned about the idiosyncrasies of our new home. With a little imagination, you can turn anything with four walls into a home. It comes down to not accepting what's in front of you, and deciding how you want to reimagine it. The new property was a corner building, which opened up so many possibilities: Did we want the front door to be on the right or the left? On Thompson or Grand Avenue? We didn't have to accept the building exactly as it was. We could create, or re-create, *anything*, just as we wanted or needed.

The original entrance, for example, was at street level, which we never considered changing until a downpour flooded our ground floor the week we were finishing 22 Thompson Street. Floods aren't unheard of in SoHo—it's one of the lowest parts of the city, Canal Street having been an actual canal. We'd been told it floods at least two times a year, a real nightmare for the poor restaurants with basements that could fill with three to four feet of water during heavy rain. But this was our first. Because we didn't have a basement, when a stretch of torrential rains came, we weren't that concerned. But the water came under the front door, into the kitchen and across the first floor.

The first time we realized we could build new

It wasn't so bad (we thought). We cleaned it up and thought we'd escaped any real damage. Two hours later we heard these strange popping noises—it was the slats of the new wood floor bowing and warping. We had to let it dry out and redo the whole thing. Thankfully, as far as other effects of the flood went, we'd followed one of our own construction rules and built a perfectly waterproof roof. And a silver lining of the flood? To prevent this from happening again, we added a front stoop to create a small barrier and some height between us and the street. The monastery gates we'd acquired, which perfectly matched the height of our old front door, had to be recut to fit the new dimensions. But we ended up loving this new entrance even more!

And what about that vacant lot next door? Even as we put the finishing touches on 22 Thompson, there was the question of what to do with that space, 24 Thompson. It was too small to build on, but too big and too ugly to just leave empty.

Our initial thought was to clean up the lot and use it to park a car. But we were full-fledged New Yorkers by this point, so we didn't *have* a car! We needed a car like someone in Montana needs subway tokens. We thought about maybe renting the lot out, letting two or three cars park there. But even that seemed like a hassle.

We thought about selling it, so we cleaned it up. We took down the barbed-wire fence so it looked less like a prison yard, and hauled out all the trash. It was so thick with debris, we went in there with rakes and went at the trash like it was wet leaves. When we finally got it looking more presentable—it was a two-week job—we almost immediately got an offer on it, for *twice* as much as we'd paid for the building!

We weren't sure what to do. The lot wasn't zoned for residential, so we technically couldn't build on it. On the other hand, if we got all the permissions and met with the community board and got it approved, *maybe* we could. But what would we possibly build there? We assumed it was too small for anything substantial. Wasn't it? And even if it wasn't, could we actually pull off a building from scratch in that spot?

I decided to find out for myself. My feet are precisely a foot long, which makes them the perfect measuring tool. I can walk a room and know exactly the width and depth. So we went next door and I walked the lot. It was twenty feet wide. Which sounds tiny at first, but the width of the average townhouse is eighteen feet. And it was approximately seventy feet deep. It was big enough! But…but what?

That's when we realized: we were intimidated only because we'd never done anything like that before. When we stood back and looked at the skinny vacant lot, it looked completely impossible, a word we rarely used. We knew it would be difficult. We had to deal with freaking *pylons*. We've always bordered on courage and naivety.

We'll get to that.

By now we knew we could trust our vision. We knew that we could put something really interesting there—plus, the challenge made us want to do it even more. But could we convince the neighbors that it was a good idea?

Rezoning a property is always difficult, but in New York City? It's a beast. It involves making a formal request to the Department of City Planning to begin a formal review called ULURP (a Uniform Land Use Review Procedure, pronounced "YOU-lurp"). And the review doesn't begin and end with the city. Since 1975, neighborhood residents have been given a bigger voice in deciding how the land around them is used, largely as a response to urban planning czar Robert Moses, who steamrolled his infrastructural projects through New York for much of the twentieth century. The old standard of "my property, my choice" is long gone, which makes sense for a city as congested as Manhattan. You want a say in whether the people building next door are going to open a business that might drastically change the neighborhood's personality. Is it another bar? A shady-looking storefront with cockfights in the basement? A mini-Target?

It makes sense in theory. But in practice, it's like the Salem witch trials, real estate edition. Any change in zoning requires public hearings involving a local community board, a borough president, and the city planning commission. Oh, and it's not just a matter of residential or commercial. Every category has subcategories, so residential districts can be classified as anything from R1 (detached single-family residences) to R10 (high-density towers). Even writing that gave me a headache; imagine what it was like to attend those meetings.

All the neighbors knew us: we were the young couple with three kids who were always playing on the sidewalk. We were the wacky newcomers who'd painted their house yellow and put flower boxes on every window. They weren't sure what to make of us. We would have to get a petition signed by all the neighbors to get this lot rezoned. And it had to happen fast: 450 signatures in forty-eight hours!

Why forty-eight hours? Well, everything had to happen fast so the powers that be could take months to deliberate. We had to go for it. We had a window of opportunity and we seized it. Finally, it was time to meet with the community board, which is composed of "energetic" individuals who have been appointed by borough presidents and have some interest in the community their board serves. Despite the signatures, they challenged us, as they are known, and allowed, to do. If you have this usable property, they broached, why not build something that would serve the whole community? A public park, for instance.

We weren't surprised by this and didn't pull any punches. We wanted to build a townhouse. We're party promoters, we told them, and we aren't afraid to put up a bar and live next door to it. It can either be a nice private home with flower boxes and children coming in and out, like our current house, or we could open a nightclub. You decide.

It wasn't the prettiest meeting, but afterward, I did what I know how to do when it comes to making nice with neighbors: I invited the community board over for cookies. I wasn't trying to beguile them with sweets. We needed them to believe what *we* believed in. We wanted them to see for themselves: "This is what we can do to a house. Now let us explain what we want to do with the space next door." We needed them to understand that even more than building a new house, we wanted to contribute to the neighborhood, to change the block's *entire character*—for the better.

Our house was a former industrial building on a street full of bars. It wasn't a tree-lined street in the West Village; it was composed of approximately 60 percent residents, 40 percent bars. And the residents didn't want another bar spitting out drunken revelers at five in the morning. It would mean more graffiti and cigarette butts galore (this was when you could smoke *anywhere* in NYC). We wanted to make the street beautiful. That was our proposal, our intent. Putting up flowers and bringing a little color to the block sets a precedent. And in the end, people were appreciative. This was an old Italian neighborhood, family oriented, and our neighbors loved that our kids were out playing in the street. That we were a family and we *lived* here. They were used to the area being a certain way, but when we showed up and started slinging yellow paint everywhere, our kids toddling around in diapers and no shoes, it warmed their hearts.

We got all the signatures. The public hearings were civil and never devolved into shouting matches. Soon our little lot was rezoned and ready to build on.

Now came the challenge that would really test our mettle: the pylons.

What, you may be wondering, are pylons? Great question! Pylons are basically pillars made of steel or concrete that are driven deep into the ground and then topped with a layer of reinforced concrete. This becomes the foundation on which the rest of the house is built. Think of them like tent stakes. You can't have a secure tent until you get those stakes planted firmly in the ground. The only difference is, pylons are tent stakes that have to be drilled a hundred feet or more into the earth, with huge machinery that rumbles angrily and wakes up every baby within a three-mile radius, shaking the ground so violently that it can shatter windows, and risks damaging the foundations of your neighbors' houses.

If our plans worked, our building at 24 Thompson would be seventy-five feet tall—the tallest single-family townhouse in downtown Manhattan. But that meant some serious pylon action. We had to install sixteen one-hundred-foot pylons in a twenty-by-seventy-foot lot surrounded by three buildings. There wasn't much margin for error. We'd been warned about the intense vibrations and accompanying potential for damage. We heard a story about an attempted pylon installation in SoHo a few decades earlier that ended up destroying two buildings in the area. It led to all kinds of lawsuits, and they had to scrap plans for construction. Twenty years later, the lot was still empty. That's the kind of campfire story that can scare the bejesus out of a home developer.

We were working with a new engineer who specialized in pylons, somebody with enough experience under his belt to know what he was doing. And he was very cautious for good reasons. We couldn't pound pylons into the ground, he told us. He suggested hydraulic drilling instead, which would cut down on the vibrations but cost twice as much. Super! Just the news every home developer wants to hear before the first wall has even been built. "Just to pour the concrete will put you two times over your budget," he told us.

One fact gave us some financial confidence: once we had it rezoned to residential, it would be worth a lot more. *A lot.* Spending more, then, could be considered a smart move rather than a total bummer.

But it wasn't the money that had us freaked out. It was the risk of damage to nearby buildings, our neighbors' buildings. We were crossing our fingers, our toes, everything we could, praying to any deity who would listen to *please please please* not let this be the end of our careers.

22 Thompson transformed

After the pylons were installed, they had to be tested—that was the scary part—and the testing was going to happen on what would turn out to be a day full of a different kind of anticipation.

Okay, so, let me set the scene. It's late November, less than a week before Thanksgiving, and we'd had to shut down our entire street for the first pylon test—yes, we were *those* people. It involved an eighty-foot-tall crane lowering a five-thousand-pound block of cement onto the pylons. If it didn't pass, we'd have to start from scratch with new pylons, and the whole mishap would set us back financially—enough that it was hard to consider the possibility of having to redo this test.

That morning, as they were preparing, I went into labor! So while we were at the hospital and I was giving birth to our fourth child, Breaker, our neighborhood was on lockdown and we were praying we weren't going to lose six figures.

I vividly remember riding home in the taxi from the hospital with newborn Breaker, nine pounds and healthy as can be, in my arms, and Robert next to us. I was eager to both bring Breaker home and find out what was happening with the pylons. We pulled up to our corner, hurried out of the cab, and shimmied through the construction barricades toward the site, baby in tow. One worker did try to discourage us, reminding us that "this is a hard-hat-only area." Normally I might have complied. But that day felt different. I was still aglow at becoming a mother (again), and we wanted to show off our healthy new baby Breaker to the crew and check on the job site. This was, after all, the family business.

Living right next door allowed us to take care of our three, then four, small kids *and* build a house from the ground up. We were blessed. Family and work were merged in a way that felt natural and exhilarating. Along with the neighbors, the team working on the building watched out for our kids as they watched what we were creating.

It was like everything converged. We passed the pylon test. We had another healthy, beautiful child. We were a family doing it our way. What other parents bring their newborn home from the hospital and straight to a construction site? But nothing about it seemed weird or out of the ordinary to us.

The pylons ultimately failed to decimate the neighborhood, and construction continued apace. We soon had a five-floor, five-thousand-square-foot townhouse with a terrace and four bedrooms with fifteen-foot ceilings and sweeping views of the city. We also added a library, a private garage, and an elevator—not necessarily because *we* needed all those amenities but because in the back of our minds, even as we still entertained notions that this might be our *new*-new "forever home," we were thinking about what a future buyer would be looking for. We put in an elevator before anybody was doing that in private residences because we realized rich people don't like to take the stairs.

But we also tried to make it uniquely our own. We painted the floors and the doors black and added a tin ceiling that we painted gold. We built a new staircase and salvaged an old mirror from the Biltmore Hotel, a building designed in the Italian Renaissance revival style that thrived for much of the twentieth century before fading out in the 1980s.

Even friends and colleagues who knew that we'd built the place from nothing still couldn't entirely believe it, invariably asking during a tour—usually by the time they hit the fourth floor—what year this clearly historic New York building had been constructed.

Next stop: Paris.

For six glorious days, my parents took us on a tour of every antique store in the City of Love. We filled a massive container with more than two hundred artifacts, everything from lighting fixtures and fabric to windows and tile. It was as if we were shipping an entire house from France to the United States, with some assembly required.

Our most exciting score was a pair of round tracery windows we found at the Clignancourt flea market, considered the biggest flea market in the world. Originally from a church in Paris, they were beautiful but old, and some rot had begun to set in. We managed to restore them and put them on the fifth floor, where they became one of the most striking parts of the whole house, visible from blocks away. It was a perfect union: New York and Paris, the Old World and the New.

Just a few months after we returned to New York from our exciting and productive trip to Paris, 9/11 happened.

There's no easy way to talk about that moment, that day. Like most Americans, I'll remember it for the rest of my life. As a mother living in Lower Manhattan, it forever changed me. It was a perfectly crisp, blue-sky day. I was getting ready to take Wolfie to preschool. We were out on the street, me and all four of the kids—Wolfgang, twins Bellamy and Tallulah, and Breaker, all three years and under. We saw the first plane fly over. It was flying low, really low, over Washington Square Park, and I watched as it hit the first tower. I thought: accident. I thought: plane crash. But our contractor, Mario, who had stepped outside, immediately knew what was going on.

"That's no accident," he said, his face white as a sheet. "Cortney, I think you and the kids should get inside *now*."

I didn't need to be told twice. I gathered the kids inside and locked the door.

I was on the fifty-eighth floor of the Chase building downtown when I saw the second plane hit. It made a boom that I felt in my bones. Everybody ran for the elevators, but I didn't feel like waiting, so I headed for the stairs and walked down the fifty-eight stories, trying not to panic, trying not to break into a run. I didn't know what was happening yet, but I knew it was very, very bad.

One of Robert's friends from Wall Street came by the house to check on us, and he started putting shoes on the kids. "We're walking to Brooklyn," he told me.

"What?" I said. "I'm not going anywhere!"

"You're coming *now*!" he insisted, his voice shaking.

"Not without Robert," I told him. And I went back outside to wait for him.

When Robert came running around the corner, we hugged like we'd never let each other go. And then we stood together, arm in arm, watching the horror unfold.

After the second building collapsed, Robert and I went back inside and stayed there through the night, listening to the screams and the fire engines outside.

The next morning, we ventured out. The air smelled of burned plastic and fuel and seared metal. Our entire block—and I'm sure every street a mile (at least) in every direction—was covered in ash. Before this day, the block already felt like a community. Many of us were on a first-name basis. But in the weeks after 9/11, it was different. People came out with hoses, with buckets, with rags, and we cleaned our neighborhood together. We stayed in communication. We offered help, food, an ear. We were a true community.

So much hugging—that's what I remember. Every New Yorker wanted to stop and give you a hug. We cheered for passing firemen and policemen. We let our children play in the street, which had so little traffic following that day. A week or so after the attacks, when we walked the streets, sat at cafés, you could feel the urgency of wanting to connect with other people, as we all tried to comprehend what had happened. We wanted to hold tight to everyone we loved. New York City has never been closer, and America has probably never been as close since.

Before 9/11, those of us on Thompson Street lived near each other, but after that awful day, we became *neighbors*. After only a few days, our construction guys were begging to come back to work. We told them not to worry, to stay home, take some time, but they insisted.

From an empty lot to a five-story walk-up with an elevator

They wanted to be useful, to find some sense of normalcy. As much as Robert and I felt more connected than ever to this place, we were still shaken. There were moments when we talked about leaving. "We're moving to Austin!" "We're moving to Montreal!" But these ideas didn't have much staying power. This was our home, and we wanted to stay. Soon enough, we were working again—and our crew was happy to be working and back together.

Even before 9/11, I'd been thinking about quitting my job. But that day changed everything. I was done pretending to be invested in the finance world, spending my days counting the minutes until I could get back to Thompson Street and see what progress had been made while I was gone all day, or join Cortney on another antique pilgrimage. So one afternoon, not long after the attacks, I made the major life decision to officially resign from the bank and brokerage firm where I'd worked for almost a decade.

Few people leave successful Wall Street jobs, but it was a declaration of what Cortney and I really wanted to do with our lives. I knew deep inside that it was the right decision, but it was still daunting, and something of a gamble. I was leaving the known for the unknown. That's scary for anyone.

We'd just rented out 22 Thompson and were prepared to move into 24 Thompson when a hedge-fund billionaire saw the house at a huge housewarming party we threw and offered a record amount of monthly rent. So much of a record that we packed up and left the next morning. Not an easy thing to do with a new baby and three toddlers. We didn't want to leave, but an opportunity is an opportunity. Where did that leave us? Living in our car, finding our next rehab project? Were we even *staying* in the city? We loved New York, but 9/11 made us wonder if maybe we wouldn't be urbanites forever. What did we really want? Was there a house out there that'd convince us to finally settle down and stay put? Is that what we even wanted?

A house in the country

2OOl

4

COUNTRY COMFORT
The Berkshires House
Great Barrington, Massachusetts

Should we stay or should we go?

Immediately after 9/11, this was the question on a lot of New Yorkers' minds, including our own. Robert and I lived just blocks away from the World Trade Center, and we watched it all in horror. We watched our homes and churches and workplaces being covered in ash.

Even when the literal smoke began to clear and the ash was more or less washed away, the smells from the aftermath still lingered in the air, along with our fear. And our sadness. And our anger. And then our fear (again). It was like that for a while, cycling through these difficult emotions each day, each hour.

My first very human reaction was to want to get out of the city—to protect my family, to find someplace safer, in case more was coming. This impulse was, I'm glad to say, very short-lived. Then I came back to myself, the self that had lived in New York long enough to feel like a New Yorker, to *be* a New Yorker. We watched the way our friends and our neighbors pulled together after this tragedy—resilient and strong—and I knew our family wasn't going anywhere. We were New Yorkers and were always going to be New Yorkers. This was our home, and we were staying put.

But a seed was planted: What would it be like to have a place outside of the city? A place in the country. Not an escape, but a retreat, a sanctuary of sorts, with a big yard. Enough grass for the kids to run through barefoot. Such a cliché daydream for parents raising their kids in the city, but it was what I was thinking! I even imagined having a country store nearby, where we could pick up groceries. Maybe there'd be nearby trails where we could walk among the trees, find some breathing room, create space for more quality family time with a gentler, less demanding routine.

So we did what any New Yorker does first when they're considering a second home: we looked east. When Robert and I were still just dating, we'd taken a few vacations in the Hamptons. Spend just five minutes there, looking out on the water, and you'll know why people love it so much. There are great restaurants, too, and people who covet the homes there just like we do wouldn't mind owning a property with hedges almost as tall as the house they encircle. But the Hamptons were way out of our price range, especially since we wanted to continue living and working in Manhattan. But once we started talking about it, we couldn't stop.

Robert and I couldn't believe that we'd made it to a point where we could talk about a *second home*, a house outside of the city that would enrich our children's lives, *our* lives. Unless you're super wealthy, a second home is a luxury. As a kid, I never knew anybody, not a single family, who owned a second home. That's something rich people had. One home is enough for anybody, right? So that's something I tried to remember when we started looking for a place in the country. Let's not get crazy. We don't need a palace. We don't need all the bells and whistles. It just needs to be practical.

We were in the midst of a conversation about buying a second home in the country, and I found myself flashing back to the modest suburban neighborhood I grew up in, in Virginia, then to milestone moments in my adult life: the debt Cortney I went into when we bought the first building in Chelsea, the two of us sitting on that dirty unfinished wood floor talking each other down from the ledge of full-blown panic. Buying the Thompson Street building in SoHo. Testing pylons so we could build a townhouse from the ground up in the empty lot next to it. Me quitting my Wall Street job. To say I felt awe and gratitude for where our lives had brought us, and the direction we were moving in, with four wonderful children—well, awe and gratitude don't begin to cover it.

So the search for our country sanctuary was on. A costume designer friend of Cortney's, Susan, owned an old renovated barn with her husband where Connecticut, New York, and Massachusetts meet up—a three-mile stretch where it feels like you're in all three states at the same time. Our first lead. GPS had yet to be invented, so we got out there with an old-fashioned Rand McNally atlas. I remembering feeling generally confused. "How are we in Massachusetts now?" I asked Cortney. "We were just in Connecticut two seconds ago!"

Susan thought we should buy the house next door to them. We loved the idea of having friends so close, but the house was on seventeen acres—remote is the word that came to mind. We both love the country, but we wanted easier access to small-town life. We wanted to be outside of the city, yes, but not so far out that we couldn't walk to the post office or a local grocer.

We didn't get the seventeen-acre property next to my friend—not just because it was out of our price range, but because we knew or hoped more kids were in our future (in addition to the four we already had!). Being closer to town felt more practical than having more house. Susan was a great cook and could whip something up on a moment's notice. I was not. I wanted to be able to get a pizza

after that two-hour drive from the city. We also didn't want everyone to retreat into their separate spaces. We wanted enough space to be together, a yard just big enough for the kids to let off steam, and plenty of things to do nearby in any season. A smaller house, with less acreage, meant less to rehab and more money available for the kids to ski and ride horses and participate in summer camp.

So while we were up there, after visiting Susan and her husband, we drove around just to see what we could see. We ended up falling in love with a town in western Massachusetts called Great Barrington, and a smaller historic hamlet right next to it called South Egremont.

Located in the scenic (and snowy-in-the-winter) Berkshires, Great Barrington and the nearby towns have so much to offer. Aside from them being just a little over two hours from both Boston and New York City, we learned that there was skiing (at Butternut and nearby Catamount), tons of hiking trails (Beartown State Forest, Monument Mountain, and Bash Bish Falls, to name just a few), and a thriving arts scene (Tanglewood, Jacob's Pillow, the Mahaiwe Performing Arts Center, Shakespeare & Company, and, in a few years' time, the Berkshire International Film Festival). Actress Karen Allen, best known for playing opposite Harrison Ford in the Indiana Jones movies, has a fiber arts business downtown. Nathaniel Hawthorne and Herman Melville began their legendary friendship on a hike nearby. The W. E. B. Du Bois Boyhood Homesite, a national historic landmark, commemorates a place of pride in the heritage of the famed civil rights activist, intellectual, and founding member of NAACP.

Though not as wildly popular as the Hamptons, over the years the Berkshires have attracted more than their fair share of A-listers, such as Leonard Bernstein, Pauline Kael, James Taylor, and Norman Mailer. A little farther north are the Clark Art Institute, MASS MOCA, and the annual Williamstown Theatre Festival. There are art galleries, clothing boutiques, and fantastic restaurants; weekly summer–fall farmers markets, food co-ops, and gourmet grocers; a handful of yoga studios;

and an independent cinema. The Berkshires offer a mix of intellectuals, artists, hippies, designers, and farmers. And it has a community where everyone really does know their neighbors on a first-name basis.

Needless to say, this was all immensely attractive to us, but we wanted to make sure we could find a house not too far from the local bustle. We knew we were spoiled by living in Manhattan, where you can literally get anything you want at any time of day or night. It's three in the morning and you need a new pair of shoes and the best slice of pie you've ever had in your life? No problem. I wanted to be able to walk to get a newspaper and a gallon of milk, and, like Cortney, after driving in from the city, I wanted to be able to order a pizza and not worry whether it was too late for delivery.

We'd get some of what we wanted, but not all of it. The building we found was not yet our dream house. It was falling apart and smaller than the one near Cortney's friends, but it had a lot of potential. It was only a mile from downtown Great Barrington, and just around the curve from the historic village of South Egremont. Shortfalls in some areas were made up for in others, for instance, by the lively and thriving energy in the south Berkshires. We didn't "discover" Great Barrington or South Egremont by any means, but we were there well before the publication of the now-famous 2012 article in *Smithsonian Magazine* naming it the best small town in the United States. So, before it grew in popularity and population, it was, relative to Manhattan, still affordable—or at least it had one house in our price range.

If only we could conquer the smell.

Oh, the smell. "Musty" is too mild a word to describe it. Like no one and nothing but the must and mildew had lived in this place for ages (and ages and ages). It was a farmhouse built in 1917 and looked as if not much had been done to it since. The walls and pine floors were so dark that they sucked up light like a black hole; the wallpaper, all eight layers of it, was soiled and peeling; the wall-to-wall carpeting from the previous owners was rotted; most of the

Good bones with a great address

The house just needed some major TLC.

bedrooms were covered in wood paneling; and the heat was shot. We were very worried that we wouldn't be able to get rid of the smell, as strong smells that have been hanging around a while can be stubborn, a tough thing to work with when renovating. There were also the remnants of the antique store that had been run by the previous owners, who had built an addition to the house. Even so, there was *something* about the place.

Part of that something was the trees—the big, old, magnificent trees. Another part was the full, flat usable acre the house sat on (room for a yard!). As far as the house went, we had to look at it with a glass-half-full perspective in order to make our final decision. We'd toured a lot of farmhouses and old homes in the area, all inviting and charming in their own way, but then we'd get to the second floor and be disappointed by the low ceilings, as if the architect couldn't imagine that someday people would be taller than me (I'm five feet, four inches). At six-three, Robert would never feel at ease in a house with ceilings so low. So the high ceilings on the second floor of our new future home were a huge plus.

Overall, the house checked a lot of boxes on our list. The high ceilings, for sure. And the windows that wrapped the whole house. The natural light was incredible, making it feel grand on a small scale. The windows also meant that even indoors we felt connected to the trees, and when the kids played in the yard and swam in the pool that we would eventually put in, Robert and I could see everything. The location was rural enough that we had neighbors with farm animals, but we also weren't far at all from downtown Great Barrington, with all the things we could, and would, do together as a family.

We learned with this project that sometimes it's much more about the property and the location than the physical building (although "good bones" are important!). We'd transformed a bland, generic, and frankly downright ugly commercial space in SoHo into a beautiful home we were proud of, so we knew we could do something magical on this New England property. The stately trees had taken a couple hundred years to look like they did. We could transform the house in a matter of months. Once we got past the smell and the depressingly dark floors and walls, we started to see how we could create something great: a fun, easy house for our family, on a budget, that we didn't have to work on every time we came up.

We didn't need it to be perfect. The house had been here for a hundred years. We just needed it to hold us and give us love, and we'd give it love back.

The day we closed on the house, before the ink was even dry on the contract, we were already ripping up the shag carpet. (Never underestimate the staying power of carpeting, especially in older homes. It usually carries odor soaked in over the years. Tear it out and suddenly you'll see a house for what it really is.) Every last inch of rug was pulled from every surface, including the staircase, where it practically crumbled in our hands after years of neglect and water damage.

This was just the beginning of our teardown. We brought our team in from the city to help with the demo and construction—and they crushed it! We'd soon knocked down all of the interior walls and gotten rid of every last appliance in the kitchen. I've never been too skilled as far as construction goes, aside from painting, but I love demoing. Like Cortney, I find it to be a great stress reliever. It was weirdly cathartic to bust down the walls. Sometimes you need the mental release of watching walls crumble. It's very therapeutic. A little time spent doing physical things, where you can switch off your brain for a bit and let your body run the show, is good for the soul.

The thick clouds of dust hanging in the air contained particles that'd probably been there since World War II. But we'd changed the home's entire personality; we weren't done with the floors, but it already felt lighter and happier (and, once the dust settled, smelled a little bit better). The next step in dealing with the smell was a fresh coat of paint on the interior. Like I told Cortney after we were done,

"If they'd just done this before the sale, they probably could've gotten twice their asking price." Very similar to the lot next to 22 Thompson Street that the owner threw in as an extra with the building, at no extra charge—if only he'd cleaned it out, he could have made far more profit. As buyers, of course, we love it. (It scares competitors and other buyers away!) All in all, a good reminder: simple cleanings and renovations can make a huge difference when trying to sell a house in disrepair.

We ended up covering the floors with a coat of white paint. Aside from the aesthetic magic it would turn out to create, it was definitely an unconventional choice. Most designers and carpenters love the look and feel of original hardwood floors and think adding anything to them is sacrilegious. But, like Robert said, it changed the whole feel of the place, brightened everything up. When the light poured in through the big windows . . . it was just gorgeous.

It wasn't entirely our idea. That's a great thing about living in New York: you're surrounded by daring designers who aren't afraid to try something new and outlandish. Around the time we bought the house, we'd noticed that a lot of loft owners in Tribeca and SoHo were painting their floors white. It doesn't just make everything brighter; it also makes a room look *bigger*. Lighter colors like white or light brown work almost like an optical illusion. The ceilings seem higher, the space in general feels roomier. It's like a magic trick that keeps on giving.

Sometimes the smallest changes can have the biggest impact. All it took in our case was a little paint, and suddenly it felt like a beach house in the mountains. If we didn't like it, we could always change it later. When you knock down a wall, that's it, the wall is gone. You've made your choice. But you can always repaint something if you change your mind.

I'm happy to report that with the simple painting solution and the DIY designs throughout the house, it's arguably the least expensive

renovation we've ever done, although it's the one that gets written about the most. It has been featured in magazines again and again, probably because what we did is more attainable than some of our other houses. We did it quickly, and the DIY projects are things most people can do with a little guidance and instruction.

But we did big things, too.

Tearing down walls to create bigger, more open rooms wasn't necessarily a new idea for us. Six tiny bedrooms upstairs were converted into four small bedrooms and one roomy master bedroom. We forgot that the kids were going to grow up and would probably be happier with bigger rooms, but we've made it work. Downstairs, the old antique store addition—clearly a trailblazer in the work-from-home movement—became part of the shared living space when we took out a wall.

Recall our resistance to the idea of trekking out to the country only to have everyone retreat to their private domains. The fewer rooms, the better, as far as we were concerned. Let everything flow, from upstairs to downstairs and out into the backyard. The former antique store became our TV room, which shared the same airspace as the kitchen, just like a New York City loft.

For this house, the best money we spent was on structural improvements. By putting in a steel beam between the edge of the kitchen and the former antique store, we opened up the whole house. The fresh coat of paint and all the new furniture and art—those are ornamental. They're fun, but they don't affect the lifespan of a house. Again, as we learned in Chelsea, the plumbing, the electrical, and any smart structural changes are where you should be putting the bulk of your investment.

There were surprises that kept things interesting. After three houses, including one built from scratch, we were pretty sure we were ready for anything. Spoiler alert: we weren't. Living in the country presented some unfamiliar challenges we could not possibly have anticipated. We didn't know what we didn't know! Like what to do if, say, a skunk gets into the house and refuses to leave. (Apparently you either leave a door open and wait for the skunk to leave on its own, or you call an animal control professional to pay a visit with a snare pole. We opted for animal control. Our city-born kids were too freaked to wait it out!) A fun fact we learned later: skunk scent kills mosquitoes, so it can come in handy—outside the house, that is.

Another surprise was some news from our plumber: we needed a new septic system. I had no idea what that even meant. I was like, "What the hell is that?" I guess some people in Manhattan have their own septic systems, but we always relied on the city sewer. So to suddenly get a bill for $6,000 when you're already on a shoestring budget...it was a shock. But if you need a new septic system, there's nothing to argue about. If you need it, you need it. We'd learned a while ago that in this line of work, you've got to roll with the punches.

We had no idea how to install a septic tank once we got it. But at least it didn't cost six grand to get rid of that stupid skunk.

Budget played a pretty huge role in almost every decision we made with this house. These constraints forced us to slow down, even when our first impulse was to act fast and get the job done. But what initially felt like a hindrance was actually, in hindsight, a blessing. I truly believe that you're not supposed to have everything all at once. Because sometimes you need to take that breath and have the time to step back and consider what you really want to do with a space.

The Berkshires house had an attic with a drop hatch. Robert and I talked about what to do with it, but we couldn't come up with something that we both liked and could also afford. So we just left it. The attic wasn't going anywhere, and there was plenty else that needed our money and attention. It was always, "We'll get to it." And that was exactly what it needed to be. We needed to let it germinate in our brains a little.

Over the years, our family kept growing and we needed more space. So we renovated the attic—put in stairs going up to it and added a bunch of beds. It became a playroom. But that took time. For a long while, we had to keep our budget in our sight line. Not that it hadn't been this way in the past, but because we weren't selling another property to buy this one, we were in a very different situation, and it resulted in design decisions that would become part of our signature style over the years. Like subway tiles. Those weren't something you'd see in a lot of nice houses, at least not at that time. But we saw them all over the place in France and Italy and Argentina, and we made a mental note of it. Sometimes you just tuck ideas away for later, even if you're not sure how or if you'll ever use them.

In the Berkshires, we had to make certain decisions fast and cheap. These kinds of restrictions—time and money—can force your creative hand and encourage the imagination. So subway tiles for all the bathrooms felt like the right way to go. I got creative in how they were used. People think they are basic, but there's nothing basic about them. And it's one of the things that always gets mentioned about the house. We had some vintage lights we'd salvaged for our last house but never used, and they worked perfectly in the new place.

We weren't in the habit of buying high-end furniture for our rehabs. We leaned more toward secondhand stuff, maybe a piece or two from IKEA. This didn't mean we didn't have expensive tastes, but the kids usually turned the furniture into pro wrestling rings—we learned the hard way that new stuff got broken in fast. You choose your battles. Where are you going to really invest your money, and where are you going to be okay with just good enough? We've never had a problem with an affordable (aka cheap) coffee table occupying the same room as a highly valuable piece of art. We still chose mindfully, of course, with the aim of creating a relaxed, comfortable, uplifting house for our time away from the city.

Just as much care was given to designing the outside, including the expansive back lawn that was nothing like we'd ever had in New York and bigger than anything I or Robert had growing up in the suburbs. I ended up doing all the landscaping myself, learning on the fly how to plant trees and create a garden we could all enjoy. I even painted the window shutters yellow. I wasn't trying to be audacious or make a statement. I just like bright, bold colors. Your house should be a *celebration*. It should scream (in a nonthreatening voice, of course), "Hey, neighbor! What a wonderful day to be alive!" We thought yellow shutters were nice. And if not? Well, we'd just paint over the yellow with something else—the easiest and cheapest of fixes. And indeed, several years later, we wanted a change and painted them rose pink, which is the color they are today.

Who knows what our neighbors were thinking during the renovation. We knew that seeing a lot of cars and vans with blue-and-white New York plates parked in the driveway incited some wariness in the hearts of the locals. That's one reason we wanted to get the construction done quickly. We were going to be living here and wanted to start our neighbor-to-neighbor relationship with as little tension as possible. This quiet little house that had sat empty for years was now filled with gruff New Yorkers tearing up everything, making a racket.

While you're doing construction, my favorite rule when it comes to new neighbors is kill 'em with kindness. And remind yourself of a couple of things: sometimes, no matter what, some may not be interested in being friends, or even getting along—you can only do your part. And by renovating, doing upgrades, rehabbing an eyesore, you're increasing everyone's property value. You're helping the neighborhood.

It can only help to go a little out of your way to make sure you connect with your closest neighbors. It's always served us very well. During construction in the Berkshires, we started getting to know our neighbors, inviting them (including their kids), over for refreshments.

I kinda loved it.

So did I. But then Wolfie went on a playdate with a friend in the neighborhood, and came home pretty upset. Apparently one of the kids told him, "My mom thinks that you have the ugliest shutters in all of Massachusetts."

I was like, "Wow. *All* of Massachusetts?"

"Mom, please, please paint them another color."

I felt bad for Wolfie, but the yellow stayed for years. I admit that the fact that our yellow shutters incited such grumbling among parents down the street felt a bit like a victory.

The final touch was the wooden fence. Not to make the property feel more suburban, but to add a little privacy and a little protection. We're just off Route 23, which can be a busy road, and our goal was to create an oasis for our kids, a place for them to grow up with freedoms they couldn't enjoy in the city. With a house covered in windows, though, and a huge backyard where our kids spent the majority of their time, we needed some kind of barrier between us and the outside world. We wanted to feel less exposed. The fence helped, and then we planted some trees and hedges around the perimeter for another layer of privacy and noise abatement.

The grass out back was enough for the kids for a while, until it wasn't.

We eventually built a pool so we wouldn't have to join a country club. When we bought the place, the broker had told us, "Oh, there's a really cute country club just down the road." When he told us the annual membership fee, we thought he was joking. Thousands of dollars to use a pool for three months out of the year and maybe play a few rounds of tennis? We've never been country club people—growing up in suburbia meant community pools and tennis courts at local schools.

Cortney and I knew we were going to use our acre of land to create something just for the kids. It didn't happen right away, not after everything we'd spent tearing down those walls. But we did eventually make our own little country club. Starting small, we created a Wiffle ball field in our backyard, followed by a basketball court in the driveway. It took a few years before we were able to discuss a pool seriously—first and foremost because we didn't yet have the money. But we also needed time. Cortney has this great saying I've always loved. "Sometimes it takes a minute," she says, "to understand how you live."

It's really true. You need to spend time in a house before you realize what you need. You can't walk in on day one and go, "I know exactly what this place is missing!" No, you don't! You just moved in. Give it time. Give yourself a chance to know the house. Give the house a chance to know you. You'll figure it out eventually.

Putting the pool in led to building an in-ground trampoline, and soon our house was a magnet for local kids looking to let off steam. We loved it. We originally put the trampoline in the ground because we liked the aesthetic, and it seemed safer. But of course our boys figured out that if they hosed it down, they could create a pretty badass slip-'n'-slide. And at one point, they built a zipline from a half-built tree house to the pool. They were living the life we'd envisioned for them, that we'd wanted for them. And we couldn't imagine a safer place for them to learn how to take risks, play, push themselves, use their imaginations.

And it was nice for us as parents because no matter where we were in the house, we could see what they were up to. Having all those windows and only an acre of property meant that whatever they were doing, we had our eye on them. That was a big weight off our shoulders.

I can't tell you exactly when I realized it, but something about this house was different. At all our other homes, if the right offer came in, we'd pack and be gone by morning. But here, we did the opposite. Rather than decorating with an eye toward a speedy exit, we leaned *into* these four walls. We happily rented it out when we knew we'd be back in the city for lengths of time—our Berkshires house was a popular summer rental long before Airbnb existed.

But we didn't design it for other people; we designed it for us. And we used it and lived in it like we expected this house, with its yellow shutters and backyard trampoline, to always be in our family.

We started using the basement and garage for storage. Over the years, we've collected all sorts of antiques and art that we don't always use immediately. These spaces became a natural place to put it all, especially when we realized that our mortgage in the Berkshires was less than half what we were paying for storage in New York. And because the house was bought and renovated in the shadow of 9/11, neither Robert nor I had any clear vision of what the future held— only that we wanted this safe haven for our family. And it's given them a sense of permanence. Everything else in their lives, every home we've moved into, they've known—because of what their parents do for a living—that it's likely temporary. But the Berkshires house...it's something special.

It's never been fear that's driven us back to this house time and time again. Sometimes it's just a need for family time. Once it was to get out of the way of Hurricane Sandy. Throughout the years we've hosted holidays there for our growing families and friends (and even our friends' families) and often find ourselves skiing on Christmas Day. Then it became a place to quarantine during the COVID-19 pandemic. Now I'm desperately trying to renovate the garage into an apartment—who knows how much more our family will grow?

Plus, as our kids become adults, this is where they can store their stuff while they figure out their place in the world. Whether they're spending a semester abroad in Ireland or moving out West to start a new job, they know that when they come back, this place will be here. It's one of the few predictable things in our crazy lives.

It's also a place they visit without us. They bring their significant others to the house to relax and have a great time. We have so many memories wrapped up in this place. Over time, it's become clear that what we love about it is that it's not precious. The windows are a little

The house became our great escape for our growing family.

crooked, in the summer lucky ladybugs visit us in the sinks. The showers work fine until everybody tries to take one at the same time. And if you slam a door too hard, the old glass hardware sometimes falls off. It's the country home we've wanted since that week following 9/11 when the seed was planted. Now the seed has sprouted and grown. It comes with a little dirt on the floor and the occasional skunk trespasser. But that's part of its charm. It has become exactly what we intended it to be: our sanctuary.

It's only been over time that I came to know for sure that this was a forever home for us. We established a couple of traditions, and they've become part of our life in this house.

The one we started just after our wedding, that's followed us to every house we've owned, has now taken over the upstairs in our Berkshires home: a wall of black-and-white family photos of all of us through the years. The photos started in the upstairs hallway and are now bursting into the bedrooms. There are too many to keep track, and I can't bring myself to take any of them down! It's a timeline of where we've been and where we're going. There are baby photos, photos from birthdays and holidays, photos of our many adventures together, photos of the kids as toddlers, then kids, then young adults, then adults. Just this week we added a photo of our daughter Bellamy's recent wedding! The collection is not carefully curated—the frames don't even match—but it feels organic and true. We look at this wall and see the messy, beautiful way life unfolds. It's not neat and it's not orderly. As the years pass and we grow as a family, so does the collection—which is why the Berkshires house is so perfect for us. It's where our hearts live. It waits for us and is here when we need it.

Another fun tradition has taken over a corner wall between the kitchen and the main eating table. Once a year, each child stands straight and tall. I take out a magic marker and slide it along the wall above each of their heads—"no standing on your tippy-toes," I remind them (yes, still)—and then next to that mark, I write their name and the date. We started this the first year we moved in, more than two decades ago; it starts low and small and has slowly climbed and grown. I am reminded, every time I look at that corner, of the profound passage of time, and how much has come and gone in the blink of an eye. Were they really that small once? Was 2005 really that long ago? It's a kind of math that connects me with the fleeting beauty of being alive, and how easily those moments you think will last forever can slip away if you're not paying attention.

A fun postscript: we've rented out the house many times over the last few decades, and we started noticing guests adding measurements of their own kids to the wall. We'd be like, "Wait, who's Max? Who's Jack?" We barely know these people, but we know that on a certain day in August of 2007, Max was four feet, three inches tall. All these memories, all the little humans who have grown up right inside these four walls, all there for posterity.

The walls can't talk, but they hold a record of our lives in photographs, in measurements. They've witnessed joys and sorrows and arguments, and witnessed our kids grow and blossom into adults. Oh, and remember that attic we created where our girls could play with their dolls? Eventually, they had their first kisses up there.

Wait, they did what now?

I'm sorry you had to find out this way, Robert.

My point is, we didn't know what that space would become. Sometimes you have to let a house reveal itself to you, and not force your vision on it. It'll tell you what it needs when the time is right.

Transforming a block downtown

2004-2007

5

ROBBING PETER
TO PAY PAUL
Centre Market Place
New York

What would you do with an entire city block?

I'm really asking.

It's one thing to make a house your own: you can paint the walls, enlarge the windows, add to the landscaping and change everything about the exterior to make it stand out. But at the end of the day, it's just one building. You can certainly influence the block with your design choices. Adding flower boxes to your front windows, as we learned on Thompson Street, can change the way your neighbors think about decorating—we added flowers, and pretty soon some neighbors were doing the same. Flowers lead to more flowers. But that influence only goes so far. If the house next door looks like it hasn't been touched in at least a half century, there's not much you can do about it. You have sovereignty over your four walls, and that's it. What the neighbors do with their homes is their business. You don't own the whole block, after all.

But what if you did?

Our favorite mode of transportation

Robert's and my favorite way to get around the city at this time was on our little white Vespa. Faster than walking, we could weave through traffic and get pretty much anywhere. As I've said, being a country girl from southern Georgia, I know my way around minibikes, dirt bikes, motorcycles—anything with wheels and an engine—so I was more than comfortable zipping through Manhattan on the Vespa. And we'd discover parts of the city that many people, even the locals, tended to miss. That's how we found what was truly magical and unique about the city. On a nice spring or summer night, we'd hop on and go find a restaurant—date night!—somewhere we'd never been. It was like being Americans in Paris! Exploring a new city, everything fresh and surprising. On the way to dinner, we'd drive down streets we'd never been on, pass buildings we'd never seen. So even when you think you know your city or town, take our advice: throw away the map (or power off the GPS) and get lost!

We're always looking for a rare find in terms of properties for sale. While some people might use one broker to real estate shop, we tend to use several—a mix of commercial and residential—since we're looking for a needle in a haystack (or more like a needle in a stack of needles). And one day, our longtime broker friend Robert Burton, who'd shown us other places over the years, suggested we swing by Centre Market Place and "give it a look."

We were intrigued. That was one street we'd never explored. I knew it was somewhere around Little Italy, or maybe NoLita (short for "north of Little Italy"), that it was home to some old gun shops— we'd find out later it was once referred to as the "gun district"—and that it was near the Old Police Headquarters building.

"Take a look at buildings one, two, four, and five," Robert told us.

"Are they selling the whole block?" I asked.

"Yep, that's exactly what's happening," he said. Building three wasn't for sale, but everything else was on the market, and from the same seller.

So it wasn't technically the whole block, but it was *most* of the block—four buildings in all. This news had our creative gears spinning. But that would be nuts to invest in *four* buildings in one fell swoop, wouldn't it?

At first we weren't even thinking financially—if we were, we might've thought twice, as they were going for over a million each. We were thinking that we'd have four buildings to do whatever we wanted with. We could really contribute to the entire personality of that block—plant trees on the street, put up 1930s-era Parisian streetlights.

We'd learned by now that location is as important, if not more so, than the property itself. And Centre Market Place is where Little Italy, Chinatown, NoLita, and SoHo all converge—it's literally in the center of all four neighborhoods. Pretty irresistible. We love a Russian proverb that has become a guiding principle: "Don't buy the house, buy the neighborhood" (or "buy the block," depending on the circumstances). You have to take everything about the location into consideration. We were faced, in this instance, with taking that credo to another level. It wasn't just "buy the block" in air quotes. We had a chance to literally *buy…the…block.*

The possibilities were mind-boggling. This wasn't just going to be a creative challenge; it would be a creative *adventure.*

To make this leap, however, we'd have to ignore one of our primary real estate rules: never buy property with existing tenants. They weren't tenants exactly—not legal tenants, anyway—but people down on their luck and squatting rent free in long-abandoned buildings. The seller, whose family had owned the properties since the 1920s, promised they'd be empty by the time we signed, should he decide to sell to us.

Because of the tenants and the shape the buildings were in, we weren't able to get a full tour of every floor. If we couldn't get the full survey of what was actually inside, which made us both a bit nervous, we at least wanted a bird's-eye view from the top. We'd always had dreams of designing a great rooftop space, and this could be the place to try out some of our ideas. So we asked the owner, Anthony Imperato, if it was possible to get up there. Anthony took one look at Cortney, who was pregnant with our second set of twins, and asked, "You, uh *sure* you want to climb up to the roof?"

And in true Cortney fashion, she was like, "Hell, yeah."

This wasn't her first rodeo.

Cortney had been pregnant for all of our renos up to that point, and it never slowed her down. She'd be up in the rafters. She'd poke around in attic spaces. She had no fear. Though we couldn't get into every room or onto every floor, we saw enough: it was a wild scene in there. You really got a sense of the place's history. For more than sixty years, from 1909 to 1973, the beautiful Old Police Headquarters building next door had served as the New York City police headquarters— we could see its famous dome from the roof—until it was converted into some of the most expensive apartments in that part of the city, inhabited by celebs like Calvin Klein, Winona Ryder, and Steffi Graf.

By this time, we'd gained some confidence in our real estate acumen when it came to purchase price versus renovation costs versus resale value. We'd learned that when it comes down to it, it's simple arithmetic, not calculus. Our new townhomes would cost a fraction per square foot in construction of what the condos in the police building cost, and would be worth a lot more per square foot than Anthony's asking price, even after construction costs. This, along with the exciting knowledge that we were getting lots of media attention (and the following that came with it), made the whole prospect seem that much more promising.

The Old Police Headquarters was the downtown place to be back in the day, the preeminent residential building for the upwardly mobile. This was long before the Jenga Tower in Tribeca and 150 Charles Street in the West Village came to be, offering concierge services, gyms, spas, and indoor pools. Having a doorman was plenty good for affluent New Yorkers back then. (I highly doubt most of today's A-listers or hedge-fund titans use the gym in their building or swim in the pool with the Smith family from 3G. I'm guessing the sellers aren't thinking about actual day-to-day living, but about selling the heck out of unnecessary excess and offering the elite a clear path to keeping up with the Joneses—the very wealthy, very famous Joneses.)

Eons before we ever heard of Centre Market Place, though, and in great contrast to what the neighborhood would become, this area was law enforcement central. We found out that 4 Centre Market Place was often referred to as "the Shack" and was where crime reporters and photographers hung out, drinking and playing cards between shifts and into the wee hours. A *New York Times* managing editor once called it the "den of the forty thieves." And the basement, we were told, had been used as a firing range, which explained (we hoped!) the slew of bullet holes in the concrete walls down there. It excited us more than fazed us. I think I remember Cortney saying about the basement that it "would make a great playroom!"

The original gun shop

Since we loved bringing history into our renovations in the form of all those vintage, secondhand, and scavenged items, we knew that if 4 Centre Market became ours, there were already layers and layers of New York City history in the mix. We loved it!

After the NYPD moved to a new headquarters near City Hall in 1973, the John Jovino Gun Shop on the bottom floor of 5 Centre Market—which held the honor of being the oldest gun shop in the United States, the biggest gun dealer in the country (in the 1980s), and (at its future location at 183 Grand Street) the last gun shop in New York City before falling victim to the COVID-19 pandemic lockdown—was featured in the film *Serpico*. The titular character (played by Al Pacino), concerned that dirty cops are coming after him, buys a Browning Hi-Power at John Jovino. The shop also made an appearance in Martin Scorsese's *Mean Streets* (also 1973), when Harvey Keitel and Robert De Niro have a fight with garbage pail lids outside the store.

Once we decided we wanted in, we began something of a courting process with the owner, Anthony Imperato. His grandfather, Frank Albanese, had bought the gun store from Mr. Jovino in the early 1920s. "When I would go there as a kid with my father," Imperato told the *New York Times* in 2000, "it was a sea of blue." So he felt some deep familial attachment to these buildings, and was protective of them. He didn't want the block turned into a bunch of condos. We needed to show him that we put care into our rehabs. We wanted him to know that we're not about mass-producing homes and quickly getting them back on the market. Every building is unique, and so it follows that every renovation is, too. We suggested that he visit our home on Thompson Street, only a handful of blocks east of Centre Market. He loved our designs. He loved the European vibe we created there. The courting was underway.

If he hadn't grown to like us, it all would've fallen apart. Thankfully, Anthony happened to be a great guy. I think it helped that we had a big family, little kids running throughout our house, filling the hallways with their energy and laughter. We told him how happy we were that his building was just a short walk from our home, so we could throw ourselves into the renovations and still be near our kids. To a family guy like Anthony, I think that made as big an impression as our designs had.

Sometimes your sales pitch isn't the main thing that helps you.

I think Anthony still had his doubts, mostly because he suspected that we didn't have enough money to afford four buildings. And he was right!

Did he ever ask us about that directly, or were we always dancing around the point?

I don't think he ever specifically said, "You guys are broke, aren't you?" But it was implied. We had to really sell him on our process. Anthony and his wife came to our Christmas party on Thompson Street, and we spent most of the night talking to him about what we wanted to do with Centre Market. We would live in the former gun shop at 5 Centre Market—it was the widest of the buildings, at twenty-six feet (which is as good as it gets in Manhattan)—because

The police building, seen through the rafters

Cortney and the construction crew

we knew we could make it feel homey fast enough to live there and tackle the rest of the buildings one by one.

We tried not to come right out and say, "We can't buy everything at once," but we had no choice. "Once we finish renovating one house and find a buyer," Robert told him, "we'll have the money to pay you for the next." It's not something any seller wants to hear. By now, though, he'd seen our work, met our kids, spent time with us, and he agreed.

I'm always a little puzzled when successful people say they are "self-made" (or when other people began referring to us that way). In most cases, and definitely in ours, everyone needs support in one way or another—sometimes in more ways than one. We had kind people like Anthony, and Joe from the Chelsea project, who worked *with* us, mentored us and supported us. It really does take a village. Trust me. We did not grow in the ways we did—as people and as a business—by pulling ourselves up by our bootstraps. I mean, we did some of that—we all have to do some of that to move forward—but it's really been our relationships with sellers, clients, brokers, brands, and even family and friends that's gotten us to where we are.

And Anthony played a huge part in that by trusting us and working with us on the Centre Market deal. His only request when we got to talking about starting renovations was, "If you find any remnants of the luncheonette that my aunt ran back in the 1950s and 1960s, would you let me know?" Sadly, we couldn't keep the famous revolver-shaped gun shop sign (he'd promised it to an advertising director in Los Angeles). But everything else was ours.

Despite Anthony generously agreeing to our deal, we still needed funding. How were we going to finance the renovation of four houses without a single buyer lined up? And why would a buyer invest in something that was currently full of trash and a basement riddled with bullet holes? Lucky for us, trash tends to scare off other buyers. The buildings were in really good shape structurally, but aesthetically they were a mess. Mostly because of all the trash. And the neglect. And the chaos created by the squatters who'd been occupying them for years. But by now you know our deal: the uglier the better—on the surface. If it's one sneeze away from collapsing, that's the wrong kind of ugly. We've learned that very few people have the vision to see past the trash to what a building can become. We never forget that a gut job is a gut job; you redo everything and anything. So while we didn't have any competition, we still needed to secure the buildings so we could sell them and get the financing to start the demo and construction.

It's all about who you know. And who the people you know know. And how to get everyone in the same room so you can make your pitch. We knew the properties were big tickets that few could afford. And the best way we knew to meet people such as these was to throw a great party.

Robert's siblings, a couple of whom lived in the city at that point, had friends who had friends, mostly working in finance. I'd spread the word in my actor and artist circles. Some sort-of-wealthy friends would bring really wealthy friends, and on and on, until the word got around and people came, then more people came, and then some more.

Robert and I had been throwing parties long before we were rehabbing houses, often in empty warehouses, but that night at 24 Thompson was one of our favorites—and it was one crazy night. Under the roof of our newly renovated townhouse that night was Suge Knight, cofounder and then CEO of Death Row records (think Dr. Dre's *The Chronic* and Snoop Dogg's *Doggystyle*) *and*, we heard, the creator of *Barney* (yes, the famous purple dinosaur) was there, too. Talk about an eclectic crowd! The party was so hopping that around two in the morning, Robert and I snuck out—the kids were at a nearby hotel with a babysitter—for coffee and a late-night breakfast at Moondance Diner on Sixth Avenue, a regular spot for us. Our party that evening rolled on and on, well into the early morning hours, and within a few days—after all the excitement, all the people who came to say hello, see the house, have a drink, do some dancing—we were ecstatic in that we had potential buyers for both properties, even though we were only hoping to sell 24 Thompson!

On top of that, we found a potential buyer for the next property that we didn't even own yet. A millionaire private investor and socialite named Brad joined the soiree that night, too. He was the ultimate bachelor: retired young, never married, no kids. So…no dependents and a bank account bursting at the seams. He told us that night, "I want one of your townhomes!" He really wanted 22 Thompson, but it sold quickly, so we promised him the next one. What we learned from that evening was that creating the energy of a home is as important as the aesthetics. For example, the people at the party that night would not remember the color of the walls but would remember the feeling they had being in the space.

It was only a few months later that we met Anthony and secured the Centre Market buildings with down payments, and called up Brad. By this point, I'd taken the leap and quit my Wall Street job, and we knew from the Thompson house sales that we had a viable business model in the works. With Brad, it worked out perfectly, as he loved the idea of buying a building that we hadn't finished rehabbing yet, a house that could be customized just for him. He wanted not just a bachelor pad but a bachelor *palace*, where he could both live alone and host parties for four hundred people (or more!). We were on board. No question. But we needed to get paid up front. A bit unconventional, sure, but doing things slightly off-kilter seemed to be what worked for us and, more or less, for our clients.

We sold 4 Centre Market to Brad at a steep discount. It was less than we would've taken normally, "normally" meaning if we had literally any money to renovate the thing without him. With Brad's up-front cash for the entire house, we were able to complete all the construction on his property and fully purchase 1 and 2 Centre Market. Sometimes all you need is one yes, and you're off to the races. We took robbing Peter to pay Paul to a whole new level.

And then came the *New York Times* story.

In September of 2004, the *Times* was about to run a short piece about us, sparked by the sale to Brad. When the photographer took our portrait, he asked about our website. Coincidentally, a business-savvy friend of Cortney's had been pushing us to build a website, but it just hadn't made it to the top of our priority list.

We shrugged it off until the photographer made an important point: "The *Times* has ten million subscribers. It's gonna be read by *a lot* of people." Then he added, "And all of them are potential customers." He was right, of course. This was a time when newspapers, especially the largest paper in the world, really mattered.

Within twenty-four hours, we had a website up. Websites in the early aughts weren't super-high-tech yet, and when you don't know anything about the internet and you need something to go live before the sun comes up and the *New York Times* hits the newsstands, your only thought is, "Put it up! Whatever! Just make sure your email address is on there somewhere!"

The article called us "world-class scavengers" and "husband-and-wife real estate developers with an eye for the unusual." The photo of the two of us standing in front of the Centre Market buildings was perhaps the best picture we'd ever had taken. Unlike some photos taken a few years later in front of the newly finished 5 Centre Market, this photo was not glitzy in the least. I'm wearing jeans and a casual shirt and holding Wolfie, who's wearing a baseball cap and throwing a peace sign at the camera. Cortney looks relaxed and is smiling, wearing a nice blouse and red pants, with a purse over her shoulder. We look like—well, like us! Maybe that's why we both like it so much. We'd been doing our thing for a few years at that point; we have no clue how to get the money to renovate, but we are smiling anyway because

left: Facade of 4 Centre Market; right: The game room of the bachelor pad

we know that somehow, some way, we will. Since we've been paving our own way, acting as if we are hopeful seems to translate, eventually, into concrete reasons to be so. We didn't even have drywall money at that point, but we smiled for the camera.

And, as luck or fate or the real estate market would have it, within a few days of the story running, we had several official offers and thousands of queries from people who wanted to buy these houses at a much bigger premium than Brad had enjoyed—houses that, it bears repeating, were at this point still abandoned buildings. From that moment on, we had a real understanding of the power of the press.

It was like a row of dominoes—Brad saying yes led to the story, which led to potential buyers lining up to buy the remaining buildings, which led to us being able to pay for the renovations of the buildings we hoped to secure without yet having the money to secure them. I wasn't crazy about the first few bids, but the proliferation

of the *New York Times* story meant we didn't have to take the first offers that came our way. We met a lot of people and had many offers, but for the first time we would be renovating properties for specific people, not just for ourselves or for some anonymous future buyer. It was more important than ever that we all liked each other and that we could collaborate on a vision for their new homes (as well as make good on our agreement with Anthony).

Building simultaneously for three next-door neighbors (we would be living at 5 Centre Market) was new territory for us. Not only did they each have their own unique ideas of what their home needed and what they wanted from it, but once we finished, we were going to be neighbors. Close neighbors. We didn't want to have people knocking on our door mistaking us for landlords.

Being discriminating in choosing the buyers paid off for us. All three were really, *really* nice. We knew from past experiences that one bad client or customer can make your life miserable, not to mention that building and construction can bring out the worst in anyone. Which is also why we needed not just a good team but a great one, to make sure the project ran as smoothly as possible.

The scope of the work and the budgets for Centre Market would be bigger than any project we'd done so far. We simply didn't have construction expertise at that level. Toward the end of the Thompson Street project, we'd put together a really good team, mostly led by two contractors (who are still with us more than two decades later). Sam, one of the two, became our general contractor for Centre Market. He knew way more about structure and mechanics than we did, so we were able to lean on him to run the show while we focused on the decorative aspects of the design. We do things a little differently than most home rehabbers—and when you're paving your own way, it's vital to have somebody who can stay with you long enough to get to know you, to be able to anticipate your needs and incorporate the decisions you've made with your client. And Sam has become that for us.

The home bar, complete with zinc top fabricated in Paris

Brad the bachelor had his own ideas of what his house should look like; it was not unlike the SoHo house: equipped with a basement screening room, a wine cellar, an expansive first floor with twelve-foot ceilings, a Juliet balcony, and a kitchen that opens up to a court-yard in the back, with a projection screen and fire pit. But Brad had opinions and suggestions for every aspect of the rehab. We asked him for magazine clippings like Robert and I had put together for our first rehab in Chelsea. But Brad wasn't the type of guy to create a mood board, nor did he want to become one. He wasn't a mood board guy—he was a bar and restaurant guy. So although I was carrying that second set of twins, Brad and I toured his favorite night-time haunts, including clubs and lounges (and bathrooms!). No way was I going to let anything slow down our hunt for Brad's designs.

He ended up loving and wanting the ocher walls he saw at Balthazar for his basement wine cellar, so we found a local painter who could reproduce that yellow-gold. The inspiration for the antique look of the wine cellar itself came from the unforgettable wine cellar at il Buco on Bond Street, once a rustic antique shop, now a renowned Italian-Mediterranean restaurant. We even found some wine racks there, which still hang in Brad's wine cellar to this day.

On the top floor, the fourth, he wanted a bar in the spirit of a French bistro. It was obvious he had something specific in mind, as he kept mentioning, "Zinc! The bar was made of zinc! It was awesome." It took a few days before Cortney finally found the zinc bar—this wasn't as easy back then—at Pastis, a French restaurant in the Meatpacking District. Instead of trying to do the guesswork of building it ourselves, we found the carpenter who'd built the one at the restaurant and hired him to re-create it. He was even able to order the zinc from the same Paris supplier he'd used for Pastis's bar.

Sometimes I had to talk Brad out of things. One example: he loved these mosaic tiles that he'd seen at a nightclub. I told him we could definitely do that, but it shouldn't cover an entire room. He pushed back, so I tried to make him understand that one wall would be more than enough. I explained that aside from being really expensive, a little would look classy, but a lot? He'd be living in a disco, and not in a cool way. He finally came around. He was going for a re-creation of a club energy in his house—and we did most of what he wanted, although Robert did have to talk him out of putting a urinal in his bathroom.

Yeah, that one was a no-go for me. I just couldn't do it. But he was a good sport about it, for sure. He trusted our expertise, which we appreciated.

If we did have a brand at this point, part of it was our trademark approach of decorating a house with eclectic finds from around the world: a newly rehabbed house, with charmingly aged and vintage objects. In this case they included an antique train station clock and a science lab desk, both from Paris; an ancient jar stand from a Buenos Aires candy shop; and lighting fixtures from South Carolina.

The game room—because c'mon, every bachelor pad needs a game room—was a favorite project for that house. We furnished it with a zebra-skin rug, a 1942 Brunswick pool table, stainless steel doors taken from the locker room of a YMCA in Philly, and a Playboy pinball machine (he really wanted the pinball machine he'd played on in the 24 Thompson Street game room—Captain Fantastic!—but after searching high and low without success, we settled on the Playboy machine, which seemed pretty fitting for an ultimate bachelor pad). The only thing I wasn't sure about was an illuminated sign we got from Anthropologie, which we put in the master bathroom. It said *TISSUS COTON*, French for "cotton fabrics." I was sure he'd reject it, telling us it was too girly or something. But he loved it.

And we came in under budget! A lot of the savings were because of the kitchen. We bought most of his kitchen right off the showroom floor from Boffi, the Italian furniture brand, at half price. When it comes to furniture, we buy floor models as often as possible. In the event there is any wear and tear, it's usually minimal, a nick here, a scratch there, easy to remedy. (And we realized very early on that you can get the same things in Queens and New Jersey and not pay Manhattan prices.)

Even better news than coming in under budget was that our first time designing in partnership with a client could not have gone better. We owe Brad a lot. It really is a form of intimacy—working with someone to design their new home, supporting them in not just articulating what they like and want, but believing in it, then helping their dreams come to life. All of this while also keeping one foot in the practical realm to ensure we stay within budget.

We tried to tie up our job with Brad on a funny note. We'd gotten to know him well enough to know one of his major fears about living in New York City: rats. We took every measure necessary to ensure he'd never come home to one scampering across the kitchen floor. He mentioned it more than once, more than twice: "No rats! Absolutely cannot have rats." So on the first night he was going to be sleeping there, while he was out, I snuck in with the key I still had and left him a present on his pillow: a beautiful, very lifelike rubber rat. "I almost had a f****** heart attack," he said the next day, smiling and shaking his head. We still laugh about it together.

So grateful for Brad—he's so much fun. And he believed in us, in what we were doing: transforming the block that his house was the start of. I'm not sure it would have happened without him. He was there at this pivotal time in our careers, when we were hitting our stride. Working on 4 Centre Market was the launching pad for what would be the beginning of our best life.

Sometimes you realize how great a certain era of your life was only by looking back on it. This was not one of those times for us—we knew without a shadow just how wonderful a time we were in while we were in it. I was in the best shape of my life, training for and running marathons. We had real money for the first time—enough that we could breathe, enjoy meals out (Sunday morning rosé and brunch at Balthazar!), and do some traveling with the whole family. We were enjoying being parents, being a family, and we were reveling in our business, in our careers.

Our location had a lot to do with all of this. During renovation of 5 Centre Market, we left the door open all the time. Friends and family were stopping by on a daily and nightly basis. We wanted to own a home where our door was always open. We wanted everything we could get in the suburbs, but we wanted it in New York. And we had it! And given that we were on the edge of SoHo and NoLita, with great food and drink nearby in those hallmark spaces where you felt like you were in another country, we didn't have a difficult time luring friends and family to stop by and say hello.

Strangers wandered in, too. Once I found a man standing in the doorway, gazing across the empty room. "What the [colorful expletive] is happening here?" he demanded, remembering the room that had once been filled with artillery.

"You must be looking for the gun shop," I told him, smiling. "They've moved."

"Wait," he said, taking a closer look, trying to take it in. "You're saying you *don't* sell guns?"

"We're building a home," I offered. "Lots of tools in here, but no guns for sale." My father was career military, but I always hated guns. I didn't have the heart to tell this man that, though, as he seemed genuinely dismayed by the disappearance of John Jovino's store. It would take months before all the old customers realized that the rumors were true and the gun shop was no more.

This was the beginning of a new era on Centre Market and the surrounding neighborhoods. It felt at times like we were living in Europe, given the architecture of that part of New York, and the restaurants. We'd chosen a place for ourselves and our kids that was exactly where we wanted to be. And by the time we started working on 5 Centre Market, our new backyard had practically given us a doctoral education in industrial design, postmodern art, and architecture. SoHo and NoLita were becoming a mecca for home and design stores. This was before it was standard to purchase a kitchen sink (or a vintage light fixture or an antique wine rack) online, so we relied on nearby stores, boutiques, and galleries that were as new to the neighborhood as we were—and not just for the actual physical things we needed, but for creative energy, for inspiration and ideas, and for the professional connections that helped us learn how to do what we were doing even better while staying true to our values, our tastes, and our vision. We were learning how to hobnob with the strong personalities at the neighborhood boutiques and shops that carried both inventory we coveted and some real attitude, and this was important for our career. But nothing was more important to us—not money or popularity or celebrity—than staying true to who we were.

The influence of our new neighborhood can't be overstated. Cool places and new brands were emerging on every block. This was the height of stores like Moss (the greatest design store that's ever existed), where our first purchase was a giant light by German designer Heike Buchfelder made of goose feathers that we hung in our master bedroom. Tory Burch's first store was a block from our new house, and Kate Spade's was just down the block from the Thompson Street townhouses. We were so curious and exhilarated—we asked questions of and engaged in conversations with the owners and employees of these stores, who felt the same passion that we did for what was emerging. The home brand that we began building was clearly inspired by our SoHo friends and colleagues. CB2 was an instant favorite of ours, and a decade later we became the first designers to collaborate and bring our own collection to life in their stores, with four major collections over two years.

We also attended parties and openings at numerous galleries and other art spaces, such as the photographer Peter Beard's gallery, not to mention Deitch Projects (1996–2010) on Grand Street, which was inspired by Andy Warhol's Factory and where I almost purchased a Keith Haring painting for a fraction of what it's worth today (regrets!). Friends like Kenny Schachter, who owned Rove Gallery, and Deborah Singer, director of the Whitney Biennial at a very young age and a walking encyclopedia of art, were formative influences on us. These galleries and the people we met there introduced us to the art world and encouraged our love for art and collecting, which would become an important part of our growth as designers.

Being immersed in this ocean of art and design, riding that rising wave, resulted in 5 Centre Market: our best house, our new home, and the one we never wanted to sell. With five floors and six thousand square feet of space, we had plenty of open terrain to play with. At 24 Thompson Street, we'd had our first install of high-end custom window treatments with the Shade Store, gorgeous red drapes, but only in the living room. It was all we could afford at the time. By the time we started the reno on 5 Centre Market, however, we were able to have custom drapes and shades on *every floor*. It was a significant moment, being in a place where we could get things done right, and a far cry from Chelsea, where my Aunt Marsha and I were sewing sections of fabric onto our existing, cheaper drapes so they'd be long enough for our new windows. We have had our own collection with the Shade Store for ten years; however, we've worked with them closely for over twenty years. They are a family-run business, just like us.

Some of our favorite additions to the house—our budget was a huge upgrade from past projects—included those treatments from the Shade Store, an oak-and-steel staircase made in Belgium, a master bedroom suite that took up the entire floor, with a soapstone Boffi bathtub and glass balcony that overlooked the street, and a stone fountain in the backyard that our team found on the French Riviera. And then...there was the roof.

Our team was talented—and getting more and more talented with each house. Skill, innovation, research, and imagination equal the ability to take on the most complex challenges. The basketball court on the roof was one of those challenges that really paid off for us as a family. It involved a massive steel dome, designed to replicate the cupola of the Old Police Headquarters across the street, and a steel mesh cover fabricated in Switzerland. Our stair guy, Antonio— bright, innovative, and a specialist in steel and welding—was key in making this happen. We designed it with Antonio, and then Antonio and I brought it to life in a parking lot in New Jersey. We

"

In the end, it wasn't just our renovations that changed the block's personality. When we moved in and our kids took over the block as their personal playground, it turned this quiet stretch of road into a vibrant little community.

Our rooftop playground

shipped it into the city on a flatbed truck, and put it in with a crane. That was an exciting day!

It's probably the best architectural build we've ever done. That famous axiom by the architect Louis Sullivan—"form follows function"—basically means that a building's style should reflect its purpose. But it can work the other way as well. Function can be the *inspiration* for form. They can coexist beautifully, becoming reflections of each other. The dome served a purpose—you could play basketball all day without worrying that you might smash a neighbor's window or lose a ball only to hear a car alarm blaring on the street below—but it also became an homage to the block's historic past.

It was mostly because of our son Wolfgang, who loved basketball, showed great promise, and was extremely dedicated. We wanted to give him someplace to practice as well as space for all the kids to play safely. It was a no-brainer for us. We spent so many summer nights up there watching Wolfie shoot hoops and Breaker climb the mesh like it was a huge jungle gym. The girls took kung fu lessons on the roof, and we had a seesaw for the smaller kids as well as a lot of open space for them to spread out and play whatever they wanted. It was a dreamy and perfect spot for our family to gather. For those moments alone, it was worth every penny.

Antonio also made us stunning glass balconies up there, similar to something we saw in Europe and took a picture of in the hopes we'd be able to include one ourselves one day. Now it was one day. He took a chance and did it. The six-foot glass railings enclosed the deck and an open-air play area, keeping the kids safe and giving us more visibility of the city with no obstructions.

In the end, it wasn't just our renovations that changed the block's personality. When we moved in and our kids took over the block as their personal playground, it turned this quiet stretch of road into a vibrant little community. More than one neighbor told us how heartening it was to see kids playing in the street again; they hadn't seen that for a long time. On some weekends, we'd unofficially close down the block for flag football—the parking garage guys would put out cones to keep the cars out—and the old Italian ladies would carry out their folding chairs to watch. Even Brad, our bachelor neighbor, would be out there on some nights, drinking a beer and cheering on the kids. It was a special time for our family that I'll always remember, not just because we were lucky enough to experience it but because we helped *build* it.

I don't just mean the houses, I mean the *community*. We were part of something special, a hidden world invisible to the rest of the city. It was a moment in time, being in that house, and we are so grateful to all the people who welcomed us.

From gun shop to family home

An old garage with great potential

6

ROOM WITH A (HIGHWAY) VIEW
400 West Street
West Village, New York

There are few words more intoxicating to a New Yorker than "curb cut."

For those unfamiliar with the phrase, please allow me to explain: in New York City, there is no parking. It simply doesn't exist. If you're on the island of Manhattan and you think you've found a parking spot, trust me, you're wrong. You either pay an arm and a leg (and then another leg and then another arm) for a parking garage or get towed, like Cortney's done probably twenty times (though I must brag, I've never gotten towed once). Even after being in New York City for a handful of years, we hadn't a clue what a curb cut was. Our go-to expediter, Steve, who knows more about New York building laws, rules, and regulations than anyone we know on the island, explained: a curb cut is a dip in a sidewalk. That's it. It allows a pedestrian to transition easily between the street and the sidewalk (effectively an on-ramp for the body) or—and this is the definition we were more interested in—lets a car drive from the street into a driveway, garage, or parking lot. To those of you outside the city, you probably know this magical thing simply as a *driveway*.

If a building has a curb cut in front of it, it basically means the property is zoned for parking and you won't have to fruitlessly circle the same mile radius over and over again. It also means you have the most coveted of New York real estate: a place to put your car. It's nearly impossible to find property in Manhattan with a curb cut. Only nine hundred homes on the whole island have one! But every once in a (long) while, a miracle comes along.

When Cortney and I toured a property in the West Village—a two-story building between Charles and Christopher Streets right next to the West Side Highway, stumbling distance from the Hudson River—it was the first thing we noticed. A house *already zoned for parking?!* What New York deity had we pleased?

Aside from the curb cut and the parking zone, however, not much about 400 West was especially impressive. Though just a block south from the famous (now infamous) Richard Meier glass-towers project, the 400 West property once housed Galaxy Auto Service, and before that, it was rumored, an S-M club. Like most off-to-the-side spots in New York, it was tied to a host of stories without much evidence. It did have a pink facade, though—an unusual choice for an auto repair shop, no? It also had an unobstructed view of the river.

Like many of our best real estate finds, our excitement wasn't about the building itself. We barely had to look inside before deciding to buy it. We didn't care if it had "good bones"; we were likely going to tear most of it down anyway. What really intrigued us was what surrounded it. "Don't buy the house, buy the neighborhood," right? The place was right in the middle of a neighborhood poised to become the next big thing.

For much of the 1980s and 1990s, the Far West Village—along the Hudson River in Lower Manhattan, between Horatio and Barrow Streets—was not a part of town in which anyone lived (anymore), much less visited. There had been a time when it was a mix of industrial-maritime buildings and residential structures, an overlap unique in Manhattan. But what was left had sadly degraded into mostly burned-out factories and warehouses, long since abandoned and fallen into disrepair.

But there were a few early hints of what the neighborhood would become. In 1997, celebrity photographer Mark Seliger bought an old auto-glass store and warehouse facing West Street and turned it into a state-of-the-art studio. Some of his most iconic subjects, Paul McCartney and Tom Wolfe among them, were photographed in that stairwell. We revel in being in the middle of creative activity, whether by fine artists or master artists and craftspeople. Wherever we built, rehabbed, renovated, and lived, we never wanted to be far from that energy. It was everything to us—two self-taught designers who wanted to keep riding that evolving wave of New York City design and to have the chance to connect with talented people who likewise responded to our work.

The real change to this neighborhood happened at the most recent turn of the century, when famed architect Richard Meier, the Pritzker Prize winner who designed the Getty Center in Los Angeles, began building a pair of high-rise residential buildings near the river. 173 and 176 Perry Street, better known as the Meier Towers, were unveiled in 2002. They were unlike anything the city had seen before: sixteen-story angular towers made almost entirely of glass with panoramic views from all sides, the epitome of modern minimalism, and a stark contrast to everything else the neighborhood had to offer. It was the kind of architecture you either loved or hated, and sometimes both. The *New York Times* called the towers "beauty queens." Filmmaker Vincent Gallo, one of the first to snatch up a condo at 173, told *Vanity Fair* that the buildings were "a microcosm of everything ugly in human beings—beautiful, beautiful architecture desecrated by scandal, greed, conniving, and gluttony."

Like every other New Yorker, we followed the story of Meier Towers with deep curiosity. Most of the public's attention was devoted to its all-glass exterior—no privacy! who could live like that?—and to the A-listers, such as Nicole Kidman, Martha Stewart, and Calvin

Klein, who ponied up millions to live in glass houses in the sky. Cortney and I were less interested in the building itself than in what it meant for the neighborhood. Was this the beginning of something? Or a fluke that would be forgotten in a few years, the area returning to its former state of urban blight?

Right around the time Meier's towers were capturing the city's attention, our friend Kenny Schachter, the world-famous art dealer of SoHo's Rove Gallery who we've mentioned as playing a key role in our modern-art education, hired artist Vito Acconci to create a permanent exhibition space and townhouse on Charles Lane, a cobblestone street a block south of the towers. Being avid art collectors by now, we spent a lot of time at Kenny's gallery, both as buyers and as friends. His excitement about what the area could become was infectious. He talked about other designers who were gravitating there—he hoped to collaborate with Baghdad-born architect Zaha Hadid, which he did a few years later—and he wasn't all that concerned that too much development would ruin the West Village's character. "You can't get stuck in some nostalgic idea of what the neighborhood *used* to be," he told the *New York Times*.

So when we happened upon our old auto shop / S-M club with the pink facade, Kenny's words were with us. The West Village was on the precipice of something huge; we just didn't know *how* huge yet. We didn't know that in 2008, just a year after we signed the deed, the Lower Manhattan waterfront would be hailed as "the new Fifth Avenue." But it would be disingenuous to say it was a complete surprise. We'd done our homework. We followed the news stories about the latest massive buildings being developed in the area. We knew that the High Line, an elevated park above Manhattan's West Side, was under construction and would open in 2009. We heard rumblings that the Whitney Museum of American Art would eventually be moving from the Breuer Building on the Upper East Side to somewhere along the Hudson River waterfront (the rumblings bore out when in 2015 the museum moved to the Meatpacking District, half a mile north of us

"

Once again, it wasn't about what the West Village *was*, but rather about what it was *becoming*. And about how we wanted to be there as it changed and flourished.

in a building designed by another Pritzker Prize winner, Italian architect Renzo Piano).

Once again, it wasn't about what the West Village *was*, but rather about what it was *becoming*. And about how we wanted to be there as it changed and flourished.

We worried that it wouldn't be as easy a sell to our kids. Wolfgang, our oldest, had just turned ten, and the younger twins, Five and Holleder, were only two. None of them were likely to be impressed with "We'll be just down the block from the Meier Towers!" But luckily, there was just enough about the neighborhood to keep them excited. We were around the corner from an amazing ice cream place and pizzeria. Their school was less than eight hundred feet away, so they could easily invite their friends home for playdates and general tomfoolery. And they would! We always wanted to be close to our kids' schools, but in this case we may have been a little *too* close, as 400 West became a popular after-school clubhouse for our kids and their friends.

The most enticing part for us grown-ups, at least in that first year, was how much freedom we had as designers. Aside from the towers and a few guys like Mark Seliger, who lived just a few doors down, we didn't have any neighbors. There was no negotiating with neighborhood subcommittees about what was or wasn't allowed, or worrying whether the people next door would complain about the noise or our design choices. We had an empty lot behind us, a closed storefront next door, and nothing but the highway and the Hudson River in front of us.

We could do whatever we wanted.

And the first thing we wanted to do was the other thing we do best: throw an epic party. I can't recommend christening a new building in this way highly enough. Whether you're gutting it or giving it a cosmetic renovation, it's the best way to bring life to a space. It's been a tradition of ours from the very beginning: before you tear down a single wall, invite your friends over for a rip-roaring soiree. This party at 400 West, where we had no electricity (we brought in

The first step? Construction party!

generators for lighting and the band), did not disappoint. (Speaking of the music, we asked guitarist Hernan Romero, one of the most brilliant musicians we've ever met, to provide tunes. He's been playing at our parties for years and never disappoints.) Five hundred people helped bless our new house, a pretty great turnout. The music and laughter from that night had only just faded when we came in with sledgehammers and started swinging.

You'd think that after all these years, the learning curve might've straightened a bit. But no, there were still new surprises to be had. Because we were building right next to a river, a *huge* river, we needed help, so we brought in the top engineer in the city, and in many ways became his students as we learned about mat foundation—or "raft" foundation, as it's sometimes called—which is basically a big slab of concrete as your base, supporting all the walls and columns. Given the soil conditions due to our proximity to the river, a mat foundation was the most durable option. And it was far easier than dealing with pylons again; the pylon installation at our second Thompson Street project still gives us nightmares.

We knew we wanted to keep the first floor as a garage. No way were we letting that curb cut go to waste. We even reinstalled the rolling door from the old Galaxy Auto Service. We wanted the history, however rumored and colorful, to be part of the new building.

We've always believed that art isn't just something you hang on a wall.

When we were deciding what to do with the rolling garage door, Kenny (who'd recently relocated to London) had an idea. He and his partner, Ilona Rich, had decided to give their brick townhouse in London a complete transformation, turning it into what they called a "fantasyland for the kids." So they asked the British artist Richard Woods—who a decade later would do a major architectural commission for the 2018 Winter Olympics in South Korea—to create floors for the basement that resembled a cartoon version of hardwood, which he constructed from printed fiberboard.

"You should see if Richard has any suggestions," Kenny told us.

Of course the facade was the perfect canvas for him, and we were already fans of his work. One of our favorites was an exhibit he created for Deitch Projects in 2002, which he called Super Tudor. Tudor-style homes, which came into popularity back in the fifteenth and sixteenth centuries, were half-timbered buildings with exposed beams. Woods crafted a mock facade for the SoHo gallery, with black-and-white half-timbering that made it look like something out of a German fairy tale.

It's an understatement to say that Woods was open to collaboration and generous with his time and talent. When we work with artists, we try not to dictate what we want or micromanage. With Woods, we asked questions, he asked questions, and then we let him do his thing. We told him what we loved about his work and that we wanted the outside of our house to be as original and stunning as the inside. We're not about minimalism or majesty, we told him, and if he could essentially *unmodernize* the building, we could be the pop of color the neighborhood needed.

A lot of people wondered why it mattered what the garage and front doors looked like. Especially since they were facing the river and the highway. Who exactly was the facade *for*? We weren't like the Meier Towers, stretching scythe-like into the sky for all of New York to see and admire. Our building was tiny and easy to miss. But when you can't compete in size, you can do so in personality.

A film clip of the ceremonial unveiling of the doors showed up later in *9 by Design*, our lively, behind-the-scenes reality show with Bravo (to which we've devoted an entire chapter; see pages 160–73). We'd let urban archaeologists dig up our backyard during the Chelsea build, so why not let a TV crew follow us around during this one? That day, we counted down and let a patched-together cardboard wall tip forward as Cortney popped the champagne and the kids cheered, to reveal Woods's vibrant blue-and-white faux-wood exterior on both the rolling garage door and the front door. A work definitely worthy of ceremony. It did exactly what we'd hoped: the house now announced itself on the increasingly crowded block. And, as a commenter on social media writes about the doors: "They make you want to see what's behind them!" It gave the house a voice and is one of my favorite art pieces we've ever commissioned.

Once we were actually living in 400 West, I obviously didn't see the facade unless I was driving into our garage. In a weird way, this made me appreciate it even more. We were, and are, honored to have worked with such an amazing collaborator. This is just one of many gratifying experiences we've had working with an incredible artist.

Because we didn't need to devote the entire garage space to parking, we turned half of it into a basketball court with herringbone hardwood. When it wasn't being used by our son Wolfie and his school pals for basketball, floor hockey, or soccer, the girls used it—once for an epic fashion show for one of their birthday parties, and another time when Cortney managed to get a bouncy house up and bouncing in there for the younger kids. Last but not least, it converted into a screening room, with a screen that dropped down in front of the basketball hoop.

That first floor was easy compared to what came next. We weren't about to compete with the Meier Towers and put up sixteen floors, but we didn't want to settle for a two-floor walk-up, either. As with every property we've worked on, we enlisted people from the very start who knew better than we did about certain aspects of a particular build. As mentioned, we had never tackled a mat foundation before. And the installation of huge glass windows for each floor—five in total (over the street-level garage)—was also a first-time adventure for us.

The second (or parlor) floor would become the kitchen, dining area, and living room, with an open floor plan moving east to west. We added an outdoor terrace, connected with a garage-type door that we could open up for a seamless indoor-outdoor flow. Didn't matter if the sun was rising or setting, we were perfectly situated to get the maximum amount of light.

The third floor was designated for the master suite—and yes, it got the entire floor. If you know nothing else about us by now, it's that we'd rather have fewer bedrooms with more square footage than a bunch of tiny bedrooms. Our family was growing by another child, and we didn't want anyone to sleep in a walk-in closet. On the fourth and fifth floors, we built four bedrooms for the kids, each one spanning the house's entire width (twenty-two and three-quarter feet, to be exact). Robert and I liked having our bedroom below the kids'. It was easier for us to watch over them if they were over us— no sneaking out possible! And at the very top, another terrace, big enough to throw some serious parties (of course!). We equipped it with a teakwood hot tub, a wood-burning fireplace, a refrigerator, a wood-burning pizza oven, and a gas barbecue.

If I had to pick the biggest challenge for this house, it was the windows—definitely the windows. Though we couldn't compete with Meier in terms of height, we followed his lead with the floor-to-ceiling glass. For any other house, especially in the city, it might not have made sense; the views aren't usually worth putting on constant display. But with 400 West, we had something priceless: an unobstructed view of the West Side Highway and the Hudson River. Regardless of how the block grew and expanded in the coming years, we'd never lose that. By the time we moved our family in, plans were already underway to have the dilapidated piers turned into public parks, so we'd never have to worry about surprise buildings going up on the piers.

Sometimes a view comes at a cost, though. The West Side Highway is interesting to look at, but it's also how seventy thousand vehicles make their way up and down Manhattan every single day. And let me tell you, getting deliveries on the West Side Highway is no easy feat. Nor was needing to block a full lane so our windows could be delivered and installed (sorry, fellow New York drivers!).

Our windows—one per floor, each standing eleven feet high and spanning the entire width of the house, twenty-three feet, plus one side window and three transoms—were not just large in dimension—they were *thick*, which meant heavy. Two-ply wouldn't be enough to block the sound, so we upgraded to three-ply, laminated *and* tempered. We spent more on the windows than on just about any other feature, and I don't regret a single penny. On a list of the city's noisiest spots published in a 2010 report in the *New York Post*, the West Side Highway ranked number three, after only the corner of 42nd and Fifth and the Bryant Park subway platform. The sound of traffic the likes of the West Side Highway does not become a soothing white noise you get used to. Try sleeping through 83 decibels of constant noise and see how long you last (I read somewhere that being exposed to anything over 85 decibels for an extended period can cause permanent hearing loss).

Among the many additional benefits of our vertically glorious windows were the maximum natural light and our ability to look down and see our kids playing safely across the street. And in one specific case, they let us witness history.

When US Airways flight 1549 made its emergency landing in the Hudson River in 2009, we were home. Though we didn't witness Captain Chesley "Sully" Sullenberger III's heroic and lifesaving landing after his plane hit a flock of geese just after takeoff, we did watch as the Airbus A320 was towed down the river. Before we knew what we were seeing, it struck us as...odd.

"Is that a *plane*?" Robert asked as we sipped our morning coffee.

I squinted for a better look. Sure enough, it looked like a plane. But what was it doing in the river?

"That doesn't seem right," I said. So we kept watching as the plane slooooooowly made its way south, like a weirdly shaped tugboat. Moments like these encapsulate the city for me: sitting next to my husband in a house we designed ourselves, fellow New Yorkers zooming by on the West Side Highway, while someone pilots a tugboat that's pulling a passenger plane downriver to deposit more than 150 people safely on the shores of the Hudson.

I didn't expect how perfect highway-and-river-adjacent living would be for our family. With so many kids, being in such close proximity to their school made our lives so much easier. It's true what Robert says, our home really did become a clubhouse, but it's also true that we loved it. And thanks to Mayor Michael Bloomberg—the greatest mayor New York has ever seen, in our opinion, having made the city safer and better with new parks all over—Pier 45, the new park directly across the West Side Highway from 400 West, opened in 2003. Just down the street, in May 2005, Pier 40 opened, the largest park built in Manhattan since Central Park, with soccer fields, basketball courts, and everything else active outdoor kids could ask for. Chelsea Piers was also booming a few blocks north. And in June 2009, the now-iconic High Line opened to great acclaim. This nearly one-and-a-half-mile-long greenway runs from the Meatpacking District through Chelsea to Thirty-Fourth Street and has played a key role in transforming the West Side. On a smaller scale, across from our new home was a beautiful paved path that wandered along the river. This new New York City was drawing more families than it had in the past. It was the most suburban experience we could find and still be in Manhattan. The kids weren't stuck inside, unable to venture out alone without adult supervision. Once they learned how to safely cross the highway, they could come and go as they pleased.

I loved to look out my window and see my kids tumble across green grass, their knees muddy, their faces full of utter joy; seeing Breaker skateboarding and the kids gathering with all their friends. The pier felt like our front yard, and our doorbell never stopped ringing. It's something we'd found for the first time in the Berkshires. We never imagined we'd find it in New York.

Naturally, we assumed that this house, more than any of the others, would be an easy sell when we were ready. It had everything going for it: parking! easy access to the highway! stellar views! We were told a few years ago that the biggest celebrity you'll ever meet is the person willing to pay you the absolute most for your home. There was a growing community of atypical buyers in New York City, and in the West Village specifically—Big Tech was coming in, including Google and Facebook. Going up directly behind us was 150 Charles Street, a former parking garage bought by one of the biggest developers in the city, who transformed it into a lavish brick-and-glass condominium that became the most expensive building on the West Side, beating out Meier Towers for cost per square foot. Also included at 150 Charles: a three-thousand-square-foot fitness center, a yoga studio, a seventy-five-foot pool, and a juice bar. With all of that, construction took close to four years, which meant that living with the sound of cranes became the norm rather than the exception.

And then Hurricane Sandy hit. On October 29, 2012, the storm came crashing upon Manhattan with waves as high as fourteen feet, and by the time it passed, it had killed forty-four people, damaged or destroyed more than sixty-nine thousand homes, and displaced thousands more New Yorkers. All told, the damage and economic loss would total $19 billion.

Tropical storms are pretty common in the South, where I come from, so some rain and winds don't faze me much, but I began to suspect this might be more than an average storm when I crossed the street to check out the river and walked right into water, *in the park*, and thought, "Well, that can't be good." I ran back to the house, shoved a few towels against the front door sill—because *that'd* surely be enough to hold back the floodwaters—and ran up to tell everyone we'd be hunkering down until the storm passed. Everyone, on this night, was me and Robert, our gang of seven, and three houseguests—my friend Laura and her two dogs.

After losing power, we crouched around candles. Losing power in New York City? Definitely historic. But we didn't think we were in any real danger. We'd built the house like a tank, anticipating a possible flood (especially after the mishap in SoHo when, during that one powerful rainstorm, water came seeping under our front door into what was then our brand-new home with brand-new wood floors). We'd used tile on the first floor—far more forgiving than wood, should water come rushing in—and we'd never even considered a basement. When water starts pooling in a basement, you've got a world of bills ahead of you. It soaks into the concrete, forming cracks that start to expand when the temperatures rise. So it's not just a musty mess that needs to be cleaned up; a waterlogged basement can damage your home's foundation. Every building has some Achilles' heel, something that will *probably* be fine if you just ignore it, and while the worst doesn't *usually* happen, it's always a good idea to plan for it anyway.

The garage level had been designed to withstand everything short of the biggest flood in the history of New York City, yet we were still a little worried—not for our lives at that point as much as for our property (our car was in the garage!). It was only when the fire department showed up and started shining their flashlights through the windows and pounding on the door, telling us we had to evacuate immediately or they'd carry us out, that we realized the true gravity of the storm. Firefighters were heroes once again, just as they were on 9/11. Our respect for them runs deep—Robert's cousin is a firefighter and we know it's a serious, life-risking job—so we didn't argue when they insisted we go with them to the police station two blocks away. From there, seven kids, two dogs, and three grown-ups piled into a police van headed to Tribeca, where Robert's brother Michael lived. The streets were deserted and eerie, but the kids were still kids, so when the driver flipped on the lights and sirens, they were thrilled! (The dogs, not so much.)

"

The best design decisions
we've ever made, the ones
that felt right and true
and are still with me today,
were the ones we made
when we were slightly
limited, either financially
or by square footage.
Those are the moments that
forced us to get creative.

Michael didn't have power either, so we had to get to his tenth-story apartment the old-fashioned way. Our bodies were pumping with adrenaline from the storm, so up we went, staircase after staircase, to be with even more family on this strange night.

The next morning, with pretty bad hangovers, Michael and I went back to assess the damage; we'd stayed up with the storm and four bottles of wine trying to soothe our anxiety about our city and my family's home. Our neighborhood was devastated. So many buildings had barely held together, and the one right next to ours had completely collapsed. We found out later that it's what drew the fire department to the neighborhood in the first place; with the winds and rain, we hadn't even known it happened. The Italian restaurant around the corner, which our kids loved and whose owner loved our kids, even letting them into the kitchen to help him cook, was totaled and never reopened. Given the tragedy that came to light in the aftermath of the storm, we considered ourselves incredibly lucky that our family was safe and that 400 West came through unscathed. The only thing that was damaged was our car, which I'd stupidly left in the garage. Otherwise, there were no broken windows, no structural damage, and no real water damage. We had built a property that was more or less seaworthy—or river-worthy, in this case.

It took a year or two for the residents and businesses on the West Side to recover from Sandy, and we found what we thought was the opportune time to sell the house. Though we put it up for sale, we ended up taking it on and off the market a few times. We had a collection of factors that weren't working in our favor: after Sandy, the real estate market hadn't followed the same path that it had after 9/11 in which it had bounced back readily. And the fear of noise from the highway and nearby construction definitely deterred some buyers (though they had not lived behind our three-ply laminated and tempered glass windows!).

We also priced the house too high, despite having come to that number honestly. Early on, about two weeks into construction, when we were putting in the mat foundation, we got a firm offer from the big developer putting up 150 Charles Street right behind us. He wanted our lot to add to his, which had a better address and direct river views. He wanted it so badly that he offered us *eight times* what we'd paid for it, an offer we obviously couldn't turn down.

The down payment went into escrow, and we were to close on it within thirty days. For legal reasons, while the potential deal was drafted, we had to stop building, and we stayed stopped for two months (a long time for us!). Then the *day before* the sale was to go through, Lehman Brothers, which was brokering it, went bankrupt. The week before that, I'd stupidly starting spending money we didn't yet have, buying a few six-figure pieces of art and design from my favorite design store, Moss, in SoHo. Just to add to the fun, the same week the deal fell through, the kids all got lice and the school put out a parents' bulletin announcing that "the family with all the kids" had lice— as if we'd started it! And I ended up in the dentist's chair getting an emergency root canal. It was an awesome week.

Getting back to how we arrived at what ended up being a too-high price: given the enormity of the offer for the lot, the *empty* lot, setting the price high on the house seemed like a no-brainer. We were (surprisingly) wrong. Simple as that. If you list a property at the right dollar amount, in hot markets you can find yourself in an exciting bidding war. But our first price simply turned out to be too high, and we had to lower it. And once you start dropping the price, you can't go back (it's painful, believe me).

Another very likely reason the house didn't sell more quickly was its lack of an elevator. We'd deemed this an unnecessary extravagance. We'd installed one at 24 Thompson as a fun extra perk, but it broke down a lot and was a snail. I could run up to the roof and back down to the street before the damn thing made it to the second floor. So we decided it was a one-time thing. But while 400 West was on the market, we rented it out to bring in needed income and had a few high-profile tenants, including the most famous actresses on the planet,

Building up with river views

followed by supermodel Heidi Klum, probably the nicest celebrity we've ever worked with. Even Jay-Z and Beyoncé had come through. All of them commented on the missing elevator. We couldn't ignore it anymore. We finally bit the bullet and put one in. This was in 2014. We ripped up the floors, added a lift big enough to hold eight people, and sold the house a week later.

It's also fair to say that by the time the house sold, most of the damage from Sandy had been repaired and a lot of the construction had died down, so the area had become more attractive to everyone, especially families. We think the elevator was the icing on the cake.

So things did not always go according to plan with this house— from rehab to (finally!) the sale. But nothing ever goes perfectly, and we learned some important lessons. We may have been overconfident about how quickly and for how much we could sell the house, but we became more confident in who we are as designers. Modern design can be beautiful—it can be bold and daring and breathtaking, and sleek and minimal, with every inch a working element of the whole—but it is extremely difficult to do perfectly. Richard Meier is a genius, and we were undeniably influenced by him, especially as we built a house in the shadow of his iconic towers. But as we learned from trying to live up to his standards, sometimes expensive doesn't always mean best.

I'm not claiming we didn't sink a lot of money into 400 West. It had by far the biggest budget of any house we'd done. And we are in awe of the designers and architects who imagined the buildings that came to define the new West Village. But we know for sure now that less really can be more. What matters is what speaks to you. What speaks to the *house*? What actually belongs there? Those are the only questions you should be asking. A sleek, minimalist, clean-line aesthetic is all well and fine, but it's not what every home needs.

The best design decisions we've ever made, the ones that felt right and true and are still with me today, were the ones we made when we were slightly limited, either financially or by square footage. Those are the moments that forced us to get creative. When we calm down and stop thinking, stop trying to fit all the pieces together perfectly, surprising and inspiring things happen. It can be more beautiful when the pieces *don't* fit together, when it feels like a building has its own fractured personality—a little bruised, with hard edges and awkward angles. The imperfections are often what gives a space its true character.

And not having the luxury of a limitless budget can force your hand in the creativity department. You are pushed to think in divergent ways. "You can't put a square peg in a round hole," as the old idiom warns. But maybe you can! If you *have* to put that square peg in the round hole because it's all you can afford, or you think the square peg is beautiful and its unusual shape complements the round hole, you might just end up with something more wonderful than anything you could've done with a sky's-the-limit budget.

Robert and I do our best with what we have. We have only our instincts to rely on, period. You just try to be the best version of yourself. We aren't Richard Meier. We aren't modernist architect Annabelle Selldorf. We're Robert and Cortney. Being the best version of ourselves means that we take risks, we go toward funky-cool and away from minimal, and we go against the grain. Sometimes we fail, we mess up, but when you're taking risks and doing things a little differently, *you are going to mess up*, no matter how much you plan and prepare and budget. What's important for us is that when we do fail, we get up, we keep going, and we keep learning and evolving. That's our superpower. What's yours?

Art Basel event designed and hosted by The Novogratz

REALITY TV
Bravo: *9 by Design*
HGTV: *Home by Novogratz*

You may have picked up on the fact that we have a hard time resisting a challenge or a new adventure. Soon after we started building the house at 400 West Street another one came knocking.

After 5 Centre Market was completed, magazines in the States and all over the world were featuring it in their pages, and this was the era when print magazines were a powerful and influential medium. Condé Nast's *Cookie* magazine did a spectacular twelve-page spread on the project and our family, followed by *Oprah* magazine, *Livingetc*, and so many more. It was like getting anointed—Condé Nast and Hearst were the gatekeepers to the big leagues, and we'd never made it past their editors before.

Then something we never anticipated happened: TV networks came a-callin'. Apparently, our work and our family would be perfect material for reality television. We didn't know much about reality TV, but Cortney and I had both loved MTV's *The Real World*, which debuted in 1992, and Bravo's *Queer Eye for the Straight Guy*. We also adored

James Lipton's *Inside the Actors Studio*—though not a reality show, it was part of the Bravo family, which was enough to make them a favorite of ours.

After meeting with all the interested networks, Bravo became our clear choice. They had an outstanding executive team, which included Lauren Zalaznick, then president of Bravo Media; Frances Berwick, soon-to-be-president of NBC Universal Women & Lifestyle Entertainment; and Andy Cohen, then vice president of original programming, responsible for *Project Runway*, *Queer Eye*, *Top Chef*, *Flipping Out*, and *Real Housewives*. Bravo seemed perfect for our urban New York City story.

Once we decided to go with Bravo and the word got out to our friends and family, a mini intervention was arranged. They thought we'd embarrass ourselves, and they were very concerned about putting the kids on television. We let them know we wouldn't put the kids in a precarious position, and that while we didn't have editing power, we would edit what came out of our mouths. We were talking a lot about building a lifestyle brand and thought a show could supercharge the opportunity. We also felt that this reality TV thing could be more powerful for us than people were giving it credit for. Worst-case scenario, we told them, we'll have some high-quality, beautifully edited home movies.

Bravo was ready for us, and we were feeling confident that they'd be great partners. And we were right.

We spent a lot of time with their team preparing for *9 by Design*, the name of our show. Andy Cohen gave us great media training, and Bravo showed a lot of concern for Cortney and the kids. They wanted Cortney to film an initial week pregnant, take six weeks off to have the baby, and then we'd return to filming full-time. They assured us that our kids would never be filmed without one of us present. They let us interview production teams ourselves and choose the one we felt most comfortable with, who would hold our best interests at heart. We chose Left Right Productions—with them, we would have full approval of the people hired to be around our kids and in our homes.

First day of filming *9 by Design* at 400 West Street

The best hire was our showrunner, Michael Selditch, who had codirected *Queer Eye* and was a former architect with a great design sense—he basically styled every shoot for our series, and brilliantly. He always had our back and made the whole experience so much fun by setting the perfect tone during filming. It helped us bond with the entire crew. Sometimes it felt like they were part of our circus, but in other moments, it felt like we were part of theirs.

We'd alert the team when we had an interesting week coming up or a particularly filmworthy day, and they would be there. With no hair or makeup required for anyone (Cortney doesn't wear makeup, nor do I, ha!), we were pretty easy, and once we got to know the crew—all very good people—we got so relaxed, we'd sometimes forget when the filming was starting and stopping. Once Cortney was still mic-ed when she went into a parent-teacher conference. The crew was careful about turning sound off when we weren't shooting. And I think we did a good job of making them relaxed and welcome in our homes while they did their job to make the show go smoothly, and to support us through the process.

Although we would film only one season with Bravo—four days a week over sixteen weeks—it resulted in eight episodes that captured some of our greatest moments that year. Our life was in full gear, and we had a blast!

For me, getting a chance to showcase our designs on TV was huge. Robert and I both grew up loving movies and television. Going to the movies would take me to faraway places where I could dream and be inspired. How fun it would be to bring art and new design ideas into someone's living room!

People always ask if reality TV is real or fake. All we can say is: our show was real. It was the most hectic time of our lives, and we didn't show a lot of the bad stuff, but aside from that, it was as real as it could get.

There were so many highlights, it's impossible to make a top ten list, or even a top twenty. As far as our reality went, we supposed there couldn't have been a better, more TV-worthy time for us as a family. But some truly memorable milestones were caught on film.

In addition to a detailed look at the build of 400 West, there was the birth of our seventh child, Major (a couple members of the film crew rode with us in the taxi on the way to the hospital). Soon after, an outstanding *New York Times* article came out about us, called "Branding the Family." The writer, Penelope Green, had attended (yes, along with our huge film crew) Major's momentous and moving christening at 400 West Street (rare for Catholics to have it in a home).

Though we'd been warned, "Be careful what you say," because the *Times* can be tough, the article could not have come out better (when we saw Penelope tearing up during the ceremony, we had a good feeling about it). She noted our "seemingly bottomless capacity for disorder and upheaval," which is fair and accurate reporting, and which we took as a compliment! She humorously wondered if our brand was that of a "gang of twenty-first-century Martha Stewarts" and described the moment when Major's just-appointed godfather, our longtime friend and former Malian basketball player Mohamed Diakite, carried him through the crowd so our guests could touch his head with blessings for Major—a tradition we've stayed true to with all seven children.

Also present were our priest, Lewis Goia, who baptized all of our kids; our friend and former tenant, the brilliant songwriter Suzanne Vega, who performed one of her original songs; and, of course, dear friends and family. The ceremony was filmed in 8mm, which gave it a slightly nostalgic home-movie look and feel.

Suffice to say, episode 3 was our favorite episode of the entire season (and of our lives that year). Also covered in *9 by Design* was the release of our first design book, *Downtown Chic: Designing Your Dream Home*, by powerhouse publisher Rizzoli, and the trip across the pond for the book launch.

That weekend in London was incredible for all of us. We arrived on a good note with a front-page spread in the *Times* of London calling us the world's coolest family, to which Wolfgang responded, "That's a lot of hype to live up to." It included a meet and greet with the UK's premier press and new friends (after a debacle with the party venue and a generous last-minute rescue by our friends Kenny Schachter and Ilona Rich). We also got to meet our friend and favorite artist Ann Carrington. We'd been a patron of hers for years but had never met in person. It was wonderful to visit her on her home turf in Margate, with her Mary Poppins vibe, and see more of her amazing work. Another highlight of our London trip was our adventure to the London Eye. Cortney and I were in one pod while the children were in another, and we communicated by walkie-talkie. Cortney and I toasted our anniversary at the top of the wheel over the River Thames. An incredibly special moment.

Once back in the States, we had the opening party for the first commercial space we'd ever designed—a huge deal for us. The Bungalow, on the Jersey Shore, was a twenty-five-thousand-square-foot, twenty-four-room luxury boutique hotel that we designed as a chic spin on the quintessential surfer shack. We really wanted to show the audience things they'd never seen before, and to see what we could do not just with a hotel room but with a whole multiuse building. Art has always been a big driving force in our storytelling as designers, and this project allowed us to showcase that to a viewing audience. The party bus from New York City to New Jersey the night of the opening—wildly documented in episode 8—was a ride to remember!

We also filmed a fun episode about Wolfgang's elite twelve-and-under basketball team where the kids helped design a fundraiser we hosted for the team, a special group of young men from all over the city—from Harlem to Bed-Stuy to Lefrak City to Westchester. The boys had been playing together since the age of eight, and ended up being the best team in the country, winning the American Athletic Union championship. Two of them—Eric Paschall and Donovan Mitchell, who were featured in the episode—found their way to the NBA, and all the kids on the team were eventually offered full college scholarships. They were great kids from great families from all over the city. It was a unique group, and representative of this priceless time in our life.

Once *9 by Design* aired, we had a very popular show on our hands. We literally were mobbed as we went about our days in New York, and even during trips elsewhere in the country. People seemed to love the show. We were getting job offers every day from people we never imagined watched Bravo, including three Oscar-winning actresses, and received endorsement deals with big companies, including Procter & Gamble, Microsoft, Old Navy, and so many more. Even our bank, First Republic, used us in their advertising—we were on billboards!

We were especially thrilled, though, when the president of the modern furniture and decor company CB2 reached out to meet about a possible multiyear collaboration. They, like almost everyone, asked the same question: When does season 2 start filming?

After a few meetings with Bravo, it became clear that with the *Housewives* franchise in full swing, if we were going to do another season, it would have to meet certain standards of drama, and a G-rated family design show would not be a good fit. We were so grateful for the experience and parted ways on excellent terms.

The issue now was that we had major deals on deck, but in order to secure them, we needed another show. This was part of our brand now—we wanted and/or needed to be on the small screen. We have found through the years that building a large brand is extremely difficult. Few can do it over the long run, as you have to keep fueling the fire. One of our design heroes, Martha Stewart, is in her eighties and still out there hustling, filming with Snoop Dogg. You gotta love it and want it—it's that simple.

The week it was determined we would not film season 2 on Bravo, HGTV got in touch. We knew very little about the shows they made, except *House Hunters*, which was on all the time. I mean, *all the time.*

We met with the then president, Kathleen Finch, and really hit it off. She had an expansive vision for her network and wanted us to be part of it. We were guaranteed a full season of thirteen thirty-minute episodes in a "before and after" format, each covering a singular project in a different home or business. This is easier said than done. On-site TV design and production is *hard.* Securing apartments and spaces in New York, where we did many of the first season's projects, meant navigating complex building rules and regulations. And the turnaround for makeovers is fast. Our projects usually take months to complete, whereas in TV reno you have a matter of days, not to mention that you must work within the constraints of an impossibly low budget.

During the first season of HGTV's *Home by Novogratz*, as we were filming for the series—constantly traveling back and forth between Manhattan and New Jersey, between Brooklyn and Hoboken, flying out to Los Angeles and back to New York—we were also doing big projects for A-list celebrities (who had no interest in being on the show) as well as raising our kids and working on developing our lifestyle brand. We were busy on every front!

Not that we were complaining. In the series, we kept our focus on what Robert and I enjoyed and what we could uniquely bring to the show. We wanted to expose viewers to all sorts of design, lots of color, lots of art, including street art and a range of more modern designs that weren't necessarily being showcased on the other house shows at the time.

In the first season, we went from designing and decorating a couple's first-time condo in Williamsburg, Brooklyn, to tackling our first-ever retail job for a four-thousand-square-foot pop-up store inside Fred Segal Santa Monica. Then back to New York to stage a crazy real estate party in the middle of its biggest snowstorm in years, then to Hoboken to update a luxury bachelor pad. We went out to LA a second time to transform an old storage room at NBA legend Paul Pierce's alma mater, Inglewood High School, into a state-of-the-art student athlete lounge, then back again to the East Coast to do a major interior design renovation— a beach house turned bohemian chic—for two sisters, both surfers, in Rockaway Beach. We did a basement makeover in the New Jersey suburbs and a refurbish of our beautiful Berkshires house that was due for some TLC. And these are but a few.

Some of the viewing audience absolutely loved it, and some did not. Our style and approach are a little bit out there, and we probably tried to do too much in certain episodes. But the popularity of *9 by Design* gave us an edge, and *Home by Novogratz* found its way to the top spot on the network's roster of design shows. We were offered another season right as season 1 was airing to big numbers.

Season 2 was very different! We had the experience of season 1 under our toolbelts and were savvier about TV design. Picking the right projects and the right clients, understanding better how to work with the budgets, and having more fluency with the rules of engagement were key. We decided to take the show on the road and invite some celebrities to either join us as consultants or volunteer their homes. So Robert and I and all of the kids were all over the country doing amazing things, meeting interesting people, and truly enjoying ourselves.

Robert and Cortney at Tony Hawk's ski house

SXSW nightclub designed by The Novogratz, Austin, Texas

Classroom at Blackbird Studios, Nashville, Tennessee, designed by
The Novogratz for John and Martina McBride with Gavin DeGraw

Season 2 included an upgrade of the 1970s ski-lodge house belonging
to legendary skateboarder Tony Hawk in Mammoth Lakes, California.
That particular trip was unforgettable. Aside from the boutique-chic-
resort makeover we did on the lodge, it was such a beautiful spot, and
Tony, a kind and warm person, generous with his time, was great with
our kids. He even took our twin boys snowboarding, which they still
talk about to this day.

We designed a club in Austin, Texas, during SXSW (South by
Southwest, the annual music, media, and film festival that packs the
city to the hilt). We fell in love with Austin and its people. We also discovered that it has some of the best antique and design stores in the
world. Uncommon Objects, which touts itself as a "one-of-a-kind emporium of transcendent junk," became a new favorite. During that job, we
were also gifted once-in-a-lifetime front-row seats to see Radiohead in
a small venue, but we fell asleep in our hotel rooms instead, because we
were so exhausted from working sixteen-hour days building and filming.

We built a classroom at Blackbird Studio in Nashville, Tennessee, for
John and Martina McBride. John, who we spent the most time with, was
one of the coolest cats we've ever met, in one of the coolest cities ever.

The Drummonds' daughters' bedroom, Pawhuska, Oklahoma

We find ourselves even now waxing nostalgic about that project and Nashville itself—what an incredible city.

We were designing in our favorite cities in America, and we even got to throw a three-day party for Microsoft at Art Basel Miami Beach, which included an elegant dinner party for fifty of the most influential people in the art world. We outfitted the table with fifty unique antique chairs, table settings, and plates, all purchased on Dixie Highway in West Palm Beach. The main event was a party for a thousand people at the Shelborne Hotel, and the band Young the Giant performed on a glass stage we built over the pool. That same night we held an auction deemed Chair-a-Palooza by the *New York Post*, selling iconic chairs (designed by Frank Gehry, Ray Eames, Philippe Starck, and others), which were then re-created by selected artists, including Rob Pruitt, Meredyth Sparks, and Sarah Morris, raising a lot of money for local art organizations.

If we had to pick a favorite episode from season 2, though, it has to be the one in Pawhuska, Oklahoma, a small city in the northern part of the state known for its prairie grasses. When our producers told us we were going to film a show in Pawhuska with someone named the Pioneer Woman, we didn't know what to say. We were intrigued yet confused, as we had never heard of the place or the person. They went on to tell us that Ree Drummond was the creator of *The Pioneer Woman*, a blog she started in 2006 (we had only a vague notion of what a blog even was) that was racking up over twenty-three million page views and four million unique visitors every month. On it, she shared updates about raising four kids (two boys and two girls) on an Oklahoma cattle ranch along with her husband, Ladd, whom she'd nicknamed the Marlboro Man. The popularity of the blog led to a cookbook a few years later, and then a show on the Food Network a couple of years after that (the power of the internet!).

We were so excited to go to Oklahoma that we brought our daughters, Bellamy and Tallulah, who were the same age as Ree and Ladd's daughters. We had a marvelous week. We stayed in Tulsa, just sixty miles south of Pawhuska, and commuted each day, the four of us, listening to the same Dixie Chicks CD over and over again. We must have played and sung along to the song "Wide Open Spaces" a hundred times that week while driving across the beautiful Oklahoma plains. It brought tears to our eyes. Like Three Dog Night sang in their iconic song "Never Been to Spain": "Well, I never been to heaven / but I been to Oklahoma."

We also came to love Tulsa with its amazing architecture, including Frank Lloyd Wright's Westhope home. Designed in the late 1920s, at 10,400 square feet, it's one of his largest residential projects and one of three Wright houses in the state. We wished we could have spent even more time exploring Tulsa and the art deco buildings it is architecturally known for, but we were there to focus on the Drummonds.

Our HGTV producers had let us know that Ree and Ladd's daughters were homeschooled and wanted a one-of-a-kind homeschool bedroom. They essentially let us do what we wanted to do with a wish list of items from the girls. In the nearby town of Jenks, Oklahoma, which had great antique stores, flea markets, and trading posts, we found some great decor for the girls' room and, of course, we brought some things back to New York.

The bedroom was a big isolated white box, which gave us limitless options. After a little research and a few inquiries, we secured a fantastic construction team, including a master carpenter who built two hanging beds that looked like something out of a fairy tale—two dream beds for two sweet girls. The beds looked almost as if they were floating and were structurally impeccable. We brought our signature use of art to the space and created a brightly colored sewing area for the kids as well as other creative spaces throughout.

The space was one of our best ever, but the highlight of the trip was hanging out on the ranch with the family—Ree and Ladd and the girls. We've maintained a warm friendship with them in the years since.

We learned in Pawhuska, and all over the United States while filming the show, as well as on different book and promotional tours, that there is great design all over our country, with talented people everywhere you choose to look. If you look for it, you will see it!

After two seasons of HGTV, we decided to move on. It was a lot of work, and we wanted to focus on our family, our brand, and new design jobs. I enjoyed every minute of this series—the filming, the work, all the families we met, and the crew, whom we got very close to. The downside was that I found myself spending time with other people's kids on set, but not my own.

One of the reasons Robert and I chose this lifestyle was so that we would have time to enjoy being a family. Some careers don't allow for that, but we were intentional, knowing from the start that we wanted a big brood. TV was so fun and such a powerful way to grow our brand. It was a moment in time that we'll remember forever.

A beach house in Brazil

7

CRYSTALS, DUNE BUGGIES, AND LEARNING TO WORK WITH WHAT YOU'VE GOT
Beach House
Trancoso, Brazil

In 2005, I was training for another New York marathon, and my ritual after running was to meet up with friends for a beer at Café Noir. I was in the best shape of my life and burning so many calories from running almost a hundred miles a week I didn't worry so much about my intake. One beer usually led to two, and so on into the evening.

On some evenings, Café Noir, which was part Cheers, part hipster hangout, was filled with the cool SoHo crowd from the fashion and art worlds. On other nights, a core group of regulars who had become my friends showed up. We'd drink and talk, drink and talk.

Gary was an advertising exec with a love of sports and pop culture, a great conversationalist who, like the rest of us, drank Stella after Stella. Chi Modu was a renowned photographer whose portraits of iconic 1990s hip-hop artists like Tupac Shakur, Mobb Deep, Eazy-E, and The Notorious B.I.G. put him on the map. (Sadly, Chi passed away from an illness in 2021, and I miss him dearly.) And then there was… we'll call him "Andrej," a Serbian architect who had a reputation for telling tall tales, especially when in his cups. He was flexible with the truth, exaggerating even when the truth was better. While the rest of us stuck to beer, he'd be downing whiskey shots like they were water. Back in the early to mid-1990s, when Chi was photographing hip-hop artists and Cortney and I were adjusting to our new life in the big city, Andrej was fighting in the Croatian War of Independence—or at least that's what he told us. He was a charmer, and we enjoyed and were amused by his stories. Most of us figured out early on that he shouldn't always be believed, like when he told us that he'd designed the famed SoHo restaurant Balthazar. It was simply too iconic of a space for him, or anyone, to casually say, "Oh, yeah, I did that." It's like saying you built the Brooklyn Bridge. We weren't buying it.

So when he told us he'd designed and owned a house in Brazil, everyone at the bar was like, "Suuuure you do."

But then he showed us pictures—actual, developed pictures (not on a phone) of him inside the house, and him outside the house with the blue, blue ocean behind him. He wasn't kidding—he really *did* have a home in South America, even if it was only half-finished. He'd bought the land and started building, then ran out of money. And now, he told us (looking right at me), he needed to unload it before he went into even more debt. His bad luck could turn out be somebody else's jackpot.

I was intrigued, but we weren't about to agree to anything until Robert and I spoke to our lawyer, who, it turns out, wasn't thrilled by the idea. It wasn't out of the realm of possibility to consider that maybe Andrej was trying to unload real estate with more problems than he was disclosing. Robert knew him, but he hadn't known him for long, and it was mostly from the bar. Even at the steep discount Andrej was offering, our lawyer reminded us that the cliché "If something seems too good to be true, it usually is" is a cliché for a reason. "Buyer beware," he said, "especially if it's in a neighborhood you need a passport to enter." Just like with Thompson Street, anything we considered buying, we wanted to make sure that there was

no ambiguity when it came to title and ownership. And in South America, our lawyer said, parameters around those things are a little more freewheelin' and ever-changing.

We decided to at least take a trip and check it out. We were sure we were probably *not* going to want it. Maybe a 15 percent chance, we told ourselves. The overseas hassle. The rehab. But as we started researching hotels that were driving distance from the house, we couldn't believe how expensive they were. The rates were right up there with what we'd once paid in Saint-Tropez on the French Riviera.

Although I should note that when we travel, we rarely stay in hotels. You can only squeeze so many people into a room, and so many kids into a bed. Our preference, especially when overseas, is to rent a house. With four boys under the age of fourteen, even if we got a deal, it'd end up costing us in the long run. If there were breakable things in those rentals, our boys were gonna find out *how* breakable. We didn't get a lot of security deposits back, let's put it that way.

The good news that came out of our hotel searches in Trancoso was the reminder that in that pre-Airbnb era, crazy-expensive hotel rooms usually meant that the property value of homes in the area would likely, eventually, catch up to the high tourist prices. In any case, Andrej agreed to meet us down there, be our host, and let us stay with him in his half-finished home. All we had to do was get there.

Easier said than done! The journey door-to-door from New York to Trancoso takes twenty hours: a nine- or ten-hour flight to São Paulo or Rio de Janeiro, typically a three-hour layover, then a second two-hour flight to Porto Seguro, then a thirty-minute ferry ride (with beer and popsicles, which help), and, finally, an hour in dune buggies on the dirt roads up to our house. You only visit this town if you really, really, reaaaaaalllly want to go there.

Traveling to Trancoso is our version of *Planes, Trains and Automobiles*, except in our case, planes, long layovers, a boat, and a Jeep. Around the time we purchased the house, there was talk of an eight-hour direct flight in the works from New York to Porto Seguro. Even had this come to fruition, which it did not, the trip would still involve a one-hour drive to Trancoso across a bumpy, uneven (but beautiful!) road that's basically red clay and dirt and can be rendered entirely unpassable by a heavy rain.

If you make it through the travel gauntlet—and it is a gauntlet—you'll discover a town that feels frozen in time, as far removed from the modern world as it's possible to find anymore. Founded by Jesuits in 1583, this sleepy fishing village survived into the twentieth century as a self-sustained ecosystem where neighbors bartered for goods and services and the outside world was entirely ignored. It didn't have electricity until 1986, and didn't get its first ATM until 2004. Without resorts, visiting cruise lines, and a vibrant nightlife, it didn't attract the average tourist. It did, however, attract hippies, who moved into town in the late seventies, bringing a funky, artisanal vibe into the mix.

After everything we've seen over the years, it takes a lot to impress us, but Cortney and I fell in love with the place immediately. The most exquisite beaches we'd ever seen—clean, wide-open, uncrowded shoreline. Bossa nova and reggae floating out into the town center from a café-restaurant. Trancoso is a slow-paced paradise, a rare corner of the globe where rustic simplicity isn't just another pose. There were millionaires there for sure, but millionaires who went to bed by nine. There weren't celebrities flying in from LA or New York, staking their claim in the newest ultra-cool playground for the rich and famous (at least not yet).

It just got better when we found Andrej's house, a sprawling plantation-style building with five spacious bedrooms and an open floor plan (our favorite!). Andrej had remarkable taste and had built a beautiful home—which we know firsthand is no easy feat. On our first walk-through, just like when we drove into Trancoso, we were bowled over. Neither Cortney nor I mentioned the knocking down of a single wall. Rare for us. When walking into a new potential buy, I usually have visions of sledgehammers dancing in my head. "That wall goes. So does that one. And I'm taking that wall down the moment they hand us the keys." But not this time. The first thing we said to each other was, "We gotta hire Andrej's contractor to finish the job." The design was set—Andrej's doing—and there was no need for us to hire a new team when we already loved what his guy was doing.

There are theories that if a beach house shows up in your dreams, you're yearning for a simpler life. We couldn't snap our fingers and transform our busy life with kids and creative careers we loved into a life on a beach in South America—but we could have a house there. We could wake up, the whole family, in a house near a pristine beach, breathe in the ocean air with our morning coffee. The thought of it made my shoulders drop an instant three inches.

When we told friends and family we were considering a place in Brazil, however, they were concerned. Was it the safest place to bring a family of young kids? The 2002 film *City of God*, much of which takes place in the slums of Rio, made an impression, and conveyed the sense that Brazil was all poverty and violence. Around the same time we were looking into buying the beach house, there was a movie in theaters called *Turistas* about some American backpackers in Brazil who get caught up in an underground organ harvesting ring. It was a great flick for horror fans, but terrible news if you worked for the Brazil tourism board.

Of course, all of those movies are fictional, not even in the ballpark of reality. Every bit of hand-wringing advice, as well intentioned as it might've been, wasn't based on any firsthand experience. Although crime was an issue in some of the larger cities of Brazil, the country's reputation for lawlessness is mostly a creation of the American media. As when you visit anywhere, use your common sense, be smart, stay aware. Learn to receive any blanket stereotypes

"

In short: never make
a major real estate
investment based on
declarations like 'I heard
from a friend of a friend
who saw it on the news.'
The only reliable source
of information is your
own two eyes and your
own two feet, being there
and experiencing a place
for yourself.

about a place or a people with healthy suspicion. Case in point: we never would have bought the buildings we did in New York if we'd listened to the worrisome advice of well-meaning friends trying to steer us clear of "danger." They were, at the time, less populated, less family-friendly neighborhoods, but it's what we could afford. Except for the most extreme cases, no place is either "totally dangerous" or "totally safe." It'll be somewhere in the middle, like life.

In short: never make a major real estate investment based on declarations like "I heard from a friend of a friend who saw it on the news." The only reliable source of information is your own two eyes and your own two feet, being there and experiencing a place for yourself.

So we decided to take the gamble—though we honestly didn't think it was much of one. The most important part of the decision, which pushed it from an "It sure would be nice" daydream into "Let's do it!" is that the math made sense. Renting out the house between our visits wouldn't just make up for what we paid for the house plus renovations and additions but result in a surplus. It was a smart, profitable investment. So it was part daydream (who wouldn't want to own their own beach house given the chance?) and part promising arithmetic. Andrej's price was a fraction of what we would've paid for an ocean beachside home in the Hamptons, which in 2005 would fetch multiple millions. This was not just a good deal, it was a really, really, really good deal. It was even a cost drop from what we'd pay in Rio de Janeiro, the tourist hot spot five hundred miles south of Trancoso. Sure, it's always risky buying in a foreign country, but it fed right into the playbook we'd written for buying properties in New York: buy in a less desirable area before the rest of the world discovers it.

It also made good economic sense for a large and growing family who wanted to travel more (since hotels were, in the end, not worth the spend). As parents, we want our kids to be exposed to cultures and landscapes far outside our own, to different ways of moving through the world, to divergent values they could learn from. We believe that traveling to and spending time in places outside of their norm can help kids grow into more compassionate human beings. And if these things could happen while we stayed in a house we loved and owned near an ocean in a peaceful town—so be it! We were also investing in the place for the friends and family who would visit.

There was so much to love about the house itself: the ocean views from the deck, the natural light, and the freedom it gifted the kids because of where it was. It was heaven on Earth for them. Like during any vacation stay anywhere, they missed their friends for a little bit, but the freedom—especially as preteens—more than made up for it. They could disappear for hours, exploring the fifteen miles of white sandy beach in either direction. They could walk into town, no shoes necessary. Freedom there is different from anywhere else: driving dune buggies, swinging on actual vines in the jungle, unfettered living. The water's so clear, you can walk into it up to your neck and still see your feet.

Trancoso's downtown also wasn't like anything they'd seen in New York or even the Berkshires. The town's center is the quadrado—Portuguese for "square"—a five-acre village green surrounded by colorful buildings, once occupied by fishermen but now by art galleries and cafés, painted in attention-grabbing shades of hot pink, cobalt blue, and daffodil yellow. The focal point of the square is the church, built in the eighteenth century with coral blocks and whalebone and framed on both sides by the sea. It's stunningly beautiful, and the perfect view on a lazy summer afternoon when you have nothing to do but munch on tapioca crepes and bowls of acai and see how long you can resist a nap.

The quadrado is always crawling with kids. Every morning and afternoon you'll find kids out there, barefoot, the boys usually shirtless, playing games of futebol (what we know in the States as "soccer"). It was a daily occurrence to watch kids kick and maneuver the ball with skills you'd only witnessed in professional athletes. We aren't exactly couch potatoes—we did, after all, build a rooftop basketball court—but we had to bring our A game to keep up in this town. My kids would spend hours playing futebol with the locals, and they're pretty good athletes, but they were no match for the local players.

At the time, we were the only Americans there, and we felt honored to be welcomed by this unique place—where every day we saw, felt, smelled, tasted things totally new to us.

That said: vacationing in a foreign land is way more relaxing and fun than owning and operating a home in that same place. Trancoso on vacation? Far easier than Trancoso as a homeowner! When you're staying at your own vacation house, there's no one to call if you have complaints or something breaks. Think twice before you purchase a piece of property on a heavenly beach after four or five margaritas.

True, it's not an easy process to buy property outside of the States, and then once you have the house, you have to maintain it year-round, even when you're not there. It's a different kind of commitment. When we bought the house, there wasn't Airbnb like there is today, but we managed it like a hotel or an Airbnb rental. We didn't do as well as we thought we would by renting it out, but in the end that was okay. The gifts it gave us—being in the town, in our home, were more than enough.

There's definitely a yin and yang to buying property off the beaten path in an area that hasn't yet been discovered by the hipsters and trendsetters. Though cars in the village are a rarity—they're banned on the quadrado—we picked up one of those Volkswagen Beetle utility vans that every 1970s hippie loved driving, and which were made exclusively in Brazil (until being discontinued in 2013). It was the perfect vehicle for driving up to the shoreline or traversing the muddy roads. We didn't *need* the car (or the dune buggy, our second big purchase after we first got there), but it was nice to have some familiar extras, especially ones that allowed us, and the kids, to get out and explore.

For us, it really became the best of all possible worlds. We had nature, but we weren't completely cut off from the world. Monkeys would come up to your window, but there was also a great sushi restaurant downtown. You could walk into a bar and get a glass of the best French wine you'd ever tasted, or a cold Brazilian beer, and there was always the chance a horse might trot in and sidle up next to you at the bar. It was the closest we ever got to glamping.

The house was move-in ready by the time we purchased it, and Andrej's taste was pretty good. Since he had been living there, we were able to move in at an affordable price—and he had done a lot of the work for us. It was a perfect situation. And as you would guess, decorating a home in a foreign country is a lot easier than building one. We made it our own to fit our aesthetic. We found local art, but it was difficult getting anything delivered. And I mean *anything*! There was no regular UPS guy to pull his truck down your dirt road every day. We tried to get a few items for the Trancoso house shipped to us only once (and that was enough!)—a container of art and small furniture pieces from New York. Aside from the debacle the delivery became, the cost was astronomical. The taxes alone—40 percent of the contents' value—were almost as much as the shipping charges. Then the container went to the wrong address. The closest city for the container delivery was Salvador, Brazil, but it somehow ended up in *El* Salvador. There were a good twenty-four hours where I seriously thought I'd need to take a road trip through the jungles of South America.

Thankfully, it finally made it to us, but it was quite the ordeal. So we figured out, okay, whatever we want to bring here from the States, it needs to come in a suitcase. Every trip from New York, we'd tell the kids, "You get to pack one change of clothes. The rest of your bag is filled with books, DVDS, silverware, curtains, pillows, whatever we can cram in there."

One of the first things I brought to the beach house, carried on my lap during the entire twenty-hour trip, was my cheap turntable and a small collection of vinyl. It's how I christened the house. I've always loved Johnny Cash, but he sounds even better played on a cheap turntable in Brazil while nursing a Jack and Coke. An enjoyable moment, but also an important one: I couldn't remember the last time I'd sat down and just listened to a record with no other distractions. That was the gift of this house. No way to pretend to be relaxing when you're really just messing around on your phone. More and more often, I found myself reflecting on what my family and I had, rather than what I *wished* we had.

Trancoso, though difficult to get to (and to get things delivered to), was paradise once we got there. What a blessing—*blessings* plural. The family dinners we've had in that house, the gatherings with new friends from town, the almost nightly soccer games we'd play as a family at the house overlooking the ocean (complete with jerseys— Brazil versus the United States!). The phone reception wasn't always great, so once cell phones came into play, the kids weren't on their devices all the time. They were on the beach. Or driving the dune buggy. We all had the chance to get away from screens, to deprogram. When we'd head back to New York, it was back to reality, but at least we'd had the experience of being exactly where we were, watching our kids get closer to one another, feeling them get closer to us. These memories alone have been worth every bit of hassle.

Definitely worth it. Because it was such a long trip, we wanted our Trancoso beach villa be our sanctuary, and to feel like it blended into the surroundings—an extension of the nature all around us. We wanted the wild monkeys and the backyard sloth to feel right at home. We also wanted it to feel uniquely *us*. More of a boutique hotel aesthetic: lots

"

There's definitely a yin and yang to buying property off the beaten path in an area that hasn't yet been discovered by the hipsters and trendsetters.

of books, lots of contemporary art from the city, mixed in with pieces we found locally, like a low-slung couch we bought from a going-out-of-business sale at a Trancoso bar. As you know, we love mixing vintage with modern, local with global.

We wanted visitors and short-term renters to come in and instantly think, "This place could only exist in Trancoso, and could only have been designed by the Novogratzes." Let that be your guide when creating your family's vacation home. How does its design reflect its surroundings—indigenous to the area, rather than something airlifted onto the property—but also *your* personality? It can be both. It *should* be both.

Our dinner table, for example, has always been a key element, a place for our family to gather at the end of the day and talk and eat—to hear how everyone is doing. And because friends and community are a vital part of our lives, we wanted a table that could accommodate a group even larger than us. Our table in Trancoso allows for twenty seats (dinner party, anyone?), and because we like our spaces open and airy, it sits in an informal, open-air "dining room" with easy access to the deck. And because our family life can be chaotic (just by way of numbers), we wanted the communal spaces to feel relaxed and fun, easy to move around in.

Even after we moved in, we were still adding to the house itself—both inside and out—and coming up with new ideas. We put in an outdoor bar, perfect for whipping up caipirinhas (Brazil's rum-based national cocktail) to cool us off on sweltering summer days. Robert's white whale was a seven-foot-tall clay-stucco pizza oven next to the bar, big enough to cook pies for any number of house-guests (pizza delivery wasn't a thing in Trancoso). For the kids, we crafted a kidney-shaped pool made with stones from a local river quarry, creating a mosaic surface that looked ragged but felt soft and soothing on bare feet. The sun warmed the rocks to perfectly heat the pool (great for night swims too!).

Dinner at home

But the pièce de résistance, the true showstopper, the thing that made it more than your average beach home in a small Brazilian village that has had electricity for only a few decades, was the tree house.

The germ of the idea came in a really unexpected way. Because we had no cable or wi-fi at the Trancoso house, anything we wanted to watch had to be physical media brought from New York. We're a family that spends a lot of time watching movies together, so we didn't scrimp when it came to setting up an entertainment center. Our TV—a large flat-screen TV, then unheard of in the area— caused such a buzz that we had regular curiosity-seekers coming to the house. Our DVD selection was limited to whatever we managed to smuggle in via our suitcases. One of those movies was the 1960 Disney movie *Swiss Family Robinson*, based on the 1812 novel by Johann David Wyss, about a shipwrecked family who builds a new life on a deserted island.

Both Robert and I grew up loving the movie. But when Breaker, our then-preteen son, watched it during one of our early visits to Trancoso, he decided it was exactly what our family was missing. He made a pretty convincing case that we should build our own tree house.

What really sold us on it, however, was when we visited a restaurant at the newly opened UXUA Casa Hotel & Spa. Located right in the main square, it was the creation of Dutch designer Wilbert Das, who'd come to Trancoso not long after we did. We were instantly charmed by his eclectic creations—twelve guesthouses painted in eggshell colors and filled with recycled and repurposed furniture. A designer after our own heart.

We met Wilbert when UXUA was being built, and one villa really caught our eye: Casa da Árvore, an eloquent, spacious guest suite crafted from recycled wood from local farms and built in a tree. When we saw the finished product—with all of Breaker's arguments still dancing in our heads—that was kinda it. Robert and I looked at each other and were both like, "We *have* to do it." We might be

the only people who've ever decided to build a small house while on vacation—and call it an even better vacation because of it.

So we hunted down the same contractors who'd built the hotel and hired them to do the same thing, on a smaller scale, on our property. The first challenge was finding a tree big enough to hold a four-hundred-square-foot space. (You know us by now; it wasn't going to be your average tree house.) It would be extra special, with a bedroom, a working bathroom, a closet, and a wraparound staircase to the second floor. It was going to be a truly inspired (and comfortable) indoor-outdoor living space. And of course, we'd do the decor and art ourselves.

There were so many new rules and guidelines that we had to learn and follow, like how far a house could be from the beach line and how visible it could be from the water. There was also the matter of approvals, which made getting building permits in New York seem like a walk in the park. The construction was 100 percent local. We used only indigenous and/or reclaimed materials like eucalyptus, tatajuba (a heavy, dense hardwood native to South and Central America), and paraju (a durable hardwood frequently used for decking and flooring, also native to South and Central America). We hired local craftspeople to put all of the pieces together.

Robert was especially captivated by the builders, who worked in a way we'd never seen in the States.

We'd hash out the designs with them, and their drawings looked weirdly crude to my American eyes. But to see the workers in action was mesmerizing. They had these archaic-looking handmade tools, because they'd created a skill set based on having no electricity. Sometimes I'd come to the site, sit down in the dirt, and just watch them work—even doing something as simple as sawing wood or putting up scaffolding—and it was like watching ballet dancers. The way

The tree house

they instinctively knew how it all would fit together, and where exactly to cut a board without needing to measure. It was all muscle memory. They'd done this work for so many years, so many *decades*, they could do it without any hesitation.

We also employed a woman named Paula, who would become a constant presence at the beach house and one of our closest allies among the locals. Andrej set us up with her when we first visited. She showed us around, got us acclimated to the surroundings, and was essentially our translator. She taught English at a nearby school and was pretty fluent in both Portuguese and English. One thing led to another, and we built an apartment over the garage for her and her partner, John, so they could live on-site and run the rental side of things when we weren't there.

When you're moving into an unfamiliar town with an unfamiliar culture, you need someone who's lived there all their life because the things you'll need won't always be a Yelp review away. Sometimes you need a person with connections, who understands the local culture and how things get done in ways you couldn't. That's true whether you're in a huge city like New York or a tiny oceanside village.

For us, that insider was Paula. When we needed help finding anything and weren't sure where to even begin, we'd ask her. Robert and I loved this local Trancoso restaurant where they'd serve their coffee in these beautiful lacquered coconut bowls. I really wanted some for our house but had no clue where to track them down. Not only was Paula familiar with the bowls, she was friendly with the artist who made them. "I'll bring you over to his studio," she told us, "and you can choose your finish."

Find your Paula, and you'll never waste another fruitless afternoon on Google.

Paula also came in handy when our house ended up getting cursed.

I'll explain this one. Because we'd be renting out the home when we weren't there, we needed a staff, more than just Paula, to make sure the property was always looking its best, inside and out. While we were interviewing potential housekeepers, not every applicant was happy that they weren't immediately offered the position. One woman we hired for a short time and then had to let go was so upset that she put a spell on the house. She officially cursed it as she stood up from the table and stormed out. In Trancoso, this actually means something. And I'm just superstitious enough that it genuinely freaked me out. Paula, however, was unfazed. She knew exactly how to lift the curse, she told us.

I woke up one morning soon after the spell was supposedly cast, and there were crystals scattered all over the front porch. Still half asleep, my first thought was that they'd all blown up from the ocean. Well, why not? We had the wild monkeys coming right up to the house, reaching their arms through the kitchen window for snacks. Why not crystals blown up from the ocean?

That's when I saw Paula placing more of them around the house. She was performing a ritual, she explained, to cast out the evil spirits, apologizing for the mess and casually mentioning that she'd hoped to finish "before either of you woke up." I don't think I could have loved Paula more at that moment. It takes a special kind of person to perform a house exorcism before making the morning coffee.

There's one problem with finding a place as magical as Trancoso. Sooner or later, the rest of the world is going to find it, too. We saw in a magazine that Beyoncé and Jay-Z fell instantly in love with the town when they visited in 2013. Beyoncé had jumped into a soccer game being played in the square, which was immortalized in the video for her song "Blue." I remember watching that video for the first time with Cortney, right in our beach house living room. We laughed and joked that we'd finally made it: Beyoncé was following us around the world! Beyoncé's sister Solange spent her honeymoon in Trancoso, and it soon became a must-see destination for celebrities like Naomi Campbell, Matthew McConaughey, and Leonardo DiCaprio. Anderson Cooper bought a beach home there in 2016. Good secrets can't stay secret forever.

In each place we've built and lived, we follow some basic, common-sense, good-person principles for living among others, especially in communities where we are clearly visitors. Be a good neighbor—warm, generous, kind. Be respectful of local traditions (the New Year celebration in Trancoso, réveillon, is not to be missed!). And above all, at least in Brazil, learn to play futebol!

Robert and Cortney at the Hollywood Castle

8

HOORAY FOR HOLLYWOOD!
The Castle
Hollywood Hills, California

In the beginning, Robert was a lot more confident than I was about a potential move across the country. We'd visited siblings out there and flown out for design jobs (mostly for television), but we'd never explored beyond a six-mile radius from wherever we were staying. Los Angeles is a massive, spread-out city, so six miles is nothing. During one trip out for an exciting project for HGTV at the Fred Segal store in Santa Monica, we'd left the East Coast during a brutal cold snap, landing in a temperate 80 degrees, and we weren't complaining, that's for sure. But even though I grew up in the Deep South and my comfort zone is definitely warm weather, I've come to love living in a place that has four distinct seasons. Besides, when deciding to move, weather is only one factor.

I need to feel a connection to the landscape, or the cityscape. I need to know our kids will be able to flourish along with Robert's and my careers. And would we be able to re-create the same aesthetic we'd developed in New York while living and working in Los Angeles? Would we be able to bring a design philosophy that was born in Manhattan to a place as utterly different and foreign (at least to us) as LA? Manhattan is on an island where your worries are your neighbors, soil, water, and a lot of deliveries. Los Angeles was built in the desert, where your concerns are hillside foundations, torrential rains (which can lead to dangerous mudslides after a drought), teeming and long-burning fires, and, of course, earthquakes.

We also hadn't had the opportunity to ditch the map, get lost, and discover the city's best-kept secrets. Our quick trips out had been short and jam-packed. And our sisters who had lived in LA had moved on by this time (back to New York!). While we had professional connections there and a handful of good friends, we'd be on our own in a way we'd never been since we had kids—almost three thousand miles away from the city we had called home for more than twenty years.

Because moving to California was mostly Robert's idea, he had some serious persuading to do. He'd joke that he liked LA so much, he even loved the strip malls. This was not helping his case!

That's true, it was my idea. But just for the record, I really was joking. I didn't *love* the strip malls. I did, however, love all the mom-and-pop stores that were still in LA, compared to Manhattan, where drugstores and banks were going up on every corner. I also had this gut feeling that New York had peaked in the real estate department and LA was on the cusp of something really cool. In recent decades, developers out there were building mostly McMansions, those cookie-cutter ideas of luxury. But things were starting to change—that's what my gut was telling me based on what I knew and what I'd seen. If we acted fast, we could be at the forefront of a new wave.

Aside from me needing to convince Cortney it was the best idea I'd had in years, a few practical challenges had to be considered. A move to the West Coast would mean at least temporarily giving up the New York team that had taken us years to assemble. A few of our people would always be with us, but not those based in Manhattan that we consulted with on a regular basis. Most of our experience leading construction projects came from the multiple television builds we'd done on our HGTV series, and television makeover is a whole different animal.

We'd have to find a new general contractor and new subcontractors. We'd be the new kids on the block with connections to forge, of the kind that took time and work to solidify in New York. The fact that we didn't have family out there anymore was sad for me, too. But I was ready for a change, and whenever we'd been out there for visits and projects, I always wanted to stay longer. I wanted to know what it would be like to actually live there, with my family. And what would it be like to design houses in LA? My curiosity and desire to grow as a designer were bigger than my fear.

Now, if I could just convince Cortney.

Robert's enthusiasm and his reasons for wanting to embark on this great experiment were admirable—I even envied him a little—but I was 100 percent resistant at the time. Los Angeles was an amazing place to spend a weekend or two, but it wasn't *home*. So that morning when, after singing the praises of California, he came out and said, "Let's move to LA," I burst into laughter. I was sure he was kidding. It was not a place I'd ever imagined myself or my family living. Ever.

Cortney's reluctance just put a fire under me. This is how we work as a couple, and as a professional team. When it comes to big decisions, we take turns taking the lead. Oftentimes she's the one who has to do the convincing. Now it was my turn. I had to find a way to show her LA through my eyes, so she could see the possibilities I saw. There was great talent out there, craftspeople we'd met who worked in the film industry, who were immensely skilled and knew how to build fast. And the space, the outdoors, the weather, the beach, seemed perfect for our rambunctious gang, who were growing up fast.

I reminded Cortney about all the amazing architecture in LA. There's the Los Angeles County Museum of Art, redesigned in 2004 by Renzo Piano; the Broad museum, designed by Diller Scofidio + Renfro, the firm responsible for the 2012 renovation of New York's Lincoln Center, who also had been part of the design team for the High Line on Manhattan's West Side; and, of course, the Getty Center, Richard Meier's masterpiece, to name a few.

Some of the biggest household-name designers on the planet also just so happened to live there full-time, among them Kelly Wearstler, Kathryn Ireland, and Rachel Ashwell, and Nate Berkus had just moved there from New York as well. This is a generalization, but also a truth: designers in Southern California make money so they can design another project so they can make more money to design another project—unlike in New York, where there are often hedge funds involved or family money. The well-to-do creatives were having a hard time at that point affording Manhattan *and* doing the work they loved. So they were living in Brooklyn, or they'd moved out West.

Like others who orient their lives around their creative pursuits—art, writing, dance, music—we are fed and sustained by practicing our craft. It's what we do, it's what we love, it's how we live. We needed to be able to keep doing it. The landscape of Manhattan had changed quite a bit by this time. The hustle had gotten harder. The city was dominated by trust-fund kids, finance professionals, and elite, uber-wealthy internationals. All of the master artisans we'd worked with over the years on different projects were getting pushed out. Shouldn't we follow them? Even if we could afford to stay in Manhattan, wouldn't it make more sense, from the point of view of our careers, to go where the talent was heading? On a basic, practical level, it would be more affordable for our big family. And each time we moved, we grew closer together, became explorers, and had fun!

In all of Robert's trying to convince me that LA was the new best place for us, the thing that really hit home and ultimately changed

"

Like others who orient their lives around their creative pursuits—art, writing, dance, music— we are fed and sustained by practicing our craft. It's what we do, it's what we love, it's how we live.

my mind came up in a text exchange. Robert was out in California, taking a few meetings about a potential TV project. We were texting nonstop, as we usually do when we're in different cities. I sent a message that I still remember word for word: "You know, we have a good life here," I typed. I was worried he'd lost a little perspective.

After just a few minutes, he texted back: "Don't be afraid to leave the good to take a shot at the great."

I didn't have a good comeback to that. I mean, obviously it wasn't quite so simple. But it was enough to make me think more seriously about it. This is partly why we make such a great pair. When one of us is nervous or afraid about a decision, the other can see all the potential benefits, the possibilities for growth. Yes, I was apprehensive about making the move—a little scared, even. We had no family, no close circle of friends in LA like we had in New York. We'd be on our own, in a manner of speaking. But I couldn't shake Robert's comment.

What if he was right? What did we have to lose? I didn't want to be the one standing in the way of our next big adventure.

Now we had to break the news to the kids and to do our best to convince *them* that making this big change wasn't the end of the world. It's one thing to jump from house to house within the same city. You don't have to say goodbye to your friends or your school, and there's not much of a learning curve. But compared to New York City? California, *Southern* California at that, may as well have been another country.

It ended up being about a fifty-fifty split. One of our teenage daughters, Bellamy, had the hardest time of all the kids—at first. She was the most in love with Manhattan. She'd miss her friends (and her winter wardrobe!). And it's heartbreaking to watch your kid struggle, especially when you know you're part of the cause. One day they'll be thankful for it, but there's a lot of time between now and "one day."

Thankfully, Cortney was so good at consoling Bellamy. Even though Cortney had managed to get on board with the move, she could relate to Bellamy's sadness and apprehension, since she wasn't entirely convinced herself. I remember her saying to our daughter, "This won't last forever," like she was saying it to herself a little bit, too. Ironically, Bellamy would end up falling in love with our new city. She'd even eventually go on to attend USC, marry an Angeleno, and start a life there. "One day" took a while, but I'm pretty sure she's not mad at us anymore.

The first step to transitioning out to the West Coast was—can you guess? Look for a house to gut! But first we had to find a rental, which we did, just a few blocks off the iconic Sunset Strip—the most renowned stretch of Sunset Boulevard, a twenty-two-mile-long road that runs between downtown LA and the ocean. While much of Sunset is super urban and gritty, the roads above it in the Hollywood Hills are quite peaceful, the neighborhoods are charming, and the area offers some of the best views in Los Angeles. Normally, a rental wouldn't be important to mention, except that this one would eventually bring us to the gem of a house we ended up buying (and gutting).

This area might not seem like an ideal spot for a family of nine, with seven kids under the age of eighteen, but this particular house had a great driveway for a basketball hoop. It had a garage that we turned into a music room, and, thank god, there was a pool. It was about as fun a place as possible for them.

The climate, the way the city (and our neighborhood) was laid out, and the absence of the kind of public transportation we were used to required an adjustment for everyone, though the longer we were there, the more we came to rely on Uber X. If we'd had to drive seven kids all over LA in that traffic, that's all we ever would have done. We had grown to love a little urban grit, so while the kids weren't easily rattled by the Sunset Strip version of city living, they were accustomed to making their way across Manhattan unchaperoned, jumping into cabs and onto subways, walking block after block. This was a huge change for them.

Eventually, we'd make our way out of LA to explore the natural magnificence of the whole of California, but in the meantime, the boys spent a lot of time enjoying the accoutrements of our rental-home additions until finding their way down to the Strip. If we'd been anywhere else in LA—where you absolutely need a car to go anywhere, not to mention the patience to sit in traffic on the 405—they would've felt trapped. But in the Hills they could just leave the house and run down to the Strip and be kids. We didn't have to watch them every second. They made Sunset their playground (they loved climbing the billboards!), their supermarket (the neighborhood bodega—the Liquor Locker—was nicer and safer than it sounds), their skate park (the hilly streets from our rental to Sunset were perfect), and their neighborhood (our kids are experts at making friends).

That friendly little bodega, Liquor Locker, was only four hundred feet from the house (that's how close the rental was to Sunset), and our kids became regulars for the candy and treats and the warm, amiable owner, whom we're still friends with to this day. The neighborhood really grew on the kids, and the part of Sunset where they hung out—and where they rarely had adult supervision—truly embraced them. They started to feel the kind of freedom to explore they'd had in Manhattan. Some normalcy began sneaking in, and they started to really enjoy themselves.

Having that freedom and flexibility, as well as nearby businesses and entertainment venues that we loved, was so important. It was the only way living in LA was going to work. We couldn't feel trapped by our surroundings, or stuck in the house because somebody else had the car and there was no way to escape without it. On some nights, we'd leave our daughters to babysit the younger boys, and Cortney and I would take Wolf and walk down to the Laugh Factory, a comedy club on Sunset Boulevard, to watch a set and grab some dinner. If the kids needed us, we could be back within minutes.

Having that freedom and flexibility, as well as nearby businesses and entertainment venues that we loved, was so important. It was the only way living in LA was going to work. We couldn't feel trapped by our surroundings, or stuck in the house because somebody else had the car and there was no way to escape without it.

To our delight, the rental house was also a stone's throw away from some iconic spots in Los Angeles, such as the Comedy Store—more historically renowned than the Laugh Factory and known as the first all-stand-up comedy nightclub in the world, having hosted such luminaries as George Carlin, Whoopi Goldberg, David Letterman, Norm Macdonald, Eddie Murphy, and on and on.

Also a few blocks away was the legendary Chateau Marmont, famous for putting up (and putting up with) some of the most famous people in Hollywood for nearly a hundred years. Robert and I loved to walk there for breakfast (we were the only walkers in our neighborhood, as far as we could tell). There's an old Hollywood saying: "If you want to be seen, go to the Beverly Hills Hotel. If you *don't* want to be seen, go to Chateau Marmont." It's where John Belushi died from an overdose, and stars like Katharine Hepburn, Warren Beatty, Paul Newman, John Wayne, and many more once temporarily called it home. The old hotel's design and decor would become a central inspiration in designing our new home (once we'd found it!).

And finding a new home—our next project—didn't come as easily as it had in New York. Though we made California friends quickly, and those friends had plenty of suggestions about where we should live, they tended to push for neighborhoods like Hancock Park, with its historic, architecturally renowned mansions, or Pacific Palisades, distinguished by its affluence and proximity to the ocean. But such heavily residential areas didn't feel quite right. We realized we didn't want to be tucked into a suburban enclave, away from everything. We did find a few areas we loved all over LA, from Hollywood to Silver Lake to Venice Beach, where a lot of New Yorkers seem to end up. After trekking all over LA trying to find a house, we came to what now seems like an obvious conclusion: that our dream house had been right down the road from us the whole time. The only area that really felt special, that made me feel excited to see what was around every corner, was right where we were, the Hollywood Hills.

Bordering Studio City and Burbank to the north and Hollywood to the south, the Hills also had the Hollywood Bowl (music is a big part of our lives), the Ford amphitheater, and the Hollywood Reservoir. It had elaborate mansions and small, funky bungalows designed by giants of architecture like John DeLario, Wallace Neff, Richard Neutra, and Frank Lloyd Wright (whose Storer House we'd end up coming to know quite well, at least from the outside).

We'd forgotten our own advice and had to go the long way around to remember it: when you're moving to a new place, especially to a really big city, narrow your options down to a neighborhood that you love—not only on paper, but based on how you feel driving through it, walking around in it. Find a great place to have coffee or dinner or a drink and ask yourself: Would you look forward to becoming a regular there?

We looked at an amazing house owned by Mitzi Shore (owner of the Comedy Store) in the Bird Streets neighborhood in Hollywood Hills, and Liza Minnelli's 5,800-square-foot mansion on Crescent Drive in Beverly Hills, a house we'd seen featured in *Architectural Digest* years before. Both were classic old Hollywood homes. Liza's was built in the 1920s and had been purchased in the 1950s by her dad, legendary film director Vincente Minnelli. I would've loved to get my hands on that place. Can you imagine what those walls have seen? It's pure Hollywood Babylon. But we just kept coming back to the truth: we loved where we were.

We started investigating this old, white, dilapidated Tudor-castle-looking house—in more technical terms, a 1920s-era turret-covered mansion in a French Normandy architectural style. We weren't immediately impressed. The turrets (conical roofs) made it look like something out of a Hollywood movie about medieval knights.

And once we got inside, it just got weirder. It was big, with 7,700 square feet of living space over three floors, seven tiny bedrooms,

and a confusing, nonsensical floor plan. It reminded me of that M. C. Escher painting *Relativity*, dizzying and slightly maniacal. It didn't have staircases crisscrossing inside a labyrinth-like interior, but it definitely read like it was designed by an architect with a penchant for cubism. It had five different styles of hardwood flooring, nine layers of white stucco, which gave it an old-highway-restaurant vibe, and a ramp that went from the back lawn into one of the upstairs bedrooms.

The current owner was a woman who'd lived there for almost half a century, mostly by herself. The house was clearly too big for one person. It had been on the market for a long time. Our theory was that no one could understand the layout or figure out how to adjust it to make it feel more homey and less labyrinthine. The broker said most people who had considered it were treating it "like a knock-down." But knocking down an old historical house wasn't for us. As he gave us the tour—as we stepped up into one room and down into another, then up again, round and round—he said, "This probably isn't for you." But he didn't know who he was talking to.

In some ways, the Castle, as we dubbed it, was similar to our house in the Berkshires, in that we loved the land it was on and the location, and knew we could make it our own on the inside. When we shifted our focus away from the details of its current interior and onto the property, which we loved, and toward the *potential* for how we might remedy the dizzying floor plan, our vision for what the house could be started to grow. We used our experience from the Berkshires house in our approach to rehabbing this house: total gut job.

A lot about it gave us pause, but just like the Berkshires house, it had a full, flat, usable backyard acre—almost unheard of in the Hills. It had an oval-shaped swimming pool (that we could, and would, transform into a saltwater pool), a parking area wide enough for five or six cars, and a three-car garage—important when thinking about

Before the transformation

resale, as it is quite the amenity in a sprawling city devoted to and reliant on car culture. Best of all, the house was built into bedrock and similar to 400 West in Manhattan in that it was built like a tank. We wouldn't have to do that part ourselves this time.

What sold me on it as much as its obvious physical assets was its location: it was quite literally in the hills—a little farther from Sunset Boulevard than our rental (six blocks versus one), and thus peaceful, quiet, and somewhat secluded. We got the idyllic life of suburbia—we'd play Wiffle ball with the kids, then take a swim and Jacuzzi—while still being close enough to Sunset that everything we could possibly need was just a walk away. The Strip was no SoHo, but it was good enough. Plus we had seven kids in a few different schools around the city—on the east side, on the west, and in the Valley. The Castle and our rental were right in the middle of most of those places.

And no small thing: during renovations, we'd get to work the way we worked in New York, where we could walk to and from the job site, go in and out all day as needed. In this line of work, time is money, and it's essential to keep things moving.

We were also pretty smitten with the other homes in our neighborhood. Diane Keaton lived down the street, and Marlon Brando was a longtime owner of the house next door. We overlooked Frank Lloyd Wright's Storer House, which our broker casually mentioned after we closed on the Castle. I didn't tell him that we would have paid a whole lot more, had we known. Not only was that historic house incredible to look down on every night, but we knew that nothing of a larger scale would be built in front of us because of it. Built in 1923, it featured a textile-block motif, its exterior concrete blocks inspired by Mesoamerican architecture, so that it almost seemed to be an extension of the natural landscape. It had fallen into disrepair during the latter half of the twentieth century, until the film producer Joel Silver bought it and paid for a full restoration.

It was the real estate history of the Castle that really captured our imagination. The house wasn't just quirky in its design; it had a back-story that could've been fodder for its own Hollywood movie. The original owner of the Castle was a celebrated and prolific silent-film actress and screenwriter named Barbara La Marr, who appeared in twenty-six films in the six-year period preceding her very early death, including *The Nut* (1921), *The Three Musketeers* (1921), *The Eternal City* (1923), and *The Girl from Montmartre* (1926). Her real life was even more colorful and scandalous than anything she portrayed on the big screen, presaging in many ways the tumultuous life of Marilyn Monroe. La Marr was a larger-than-life Hollywood starlet who had fierce ambition, terrible taste in men, and self-destructive tendencies. By age nineteen, she'd been married three times—wild, illegal, and/or tragic marriages, each one ending in either divorce or widowhood. She developed a drug addiction after spraining her ankle while film-ing and died at just twenty-nine years of age. She is famously quoted as saying: "I take lovers like roses: by the dozen."

Lovers by the dozen? Maybe *that's* why the Castle had so many bedrooms.

When the sale was final and we started planning the reno, we wondered if once we started tearing things apart, we might find arti-facts or mementos left behind by the original owner. Surely a woman with La Marr's reputation had a few secrets stashed in those walls, right? Though we're not sure who they belonged to, we did find some incredible old black-and-white photographs and several dozen rusty film reel canisters (because we had no way to watch them, we donated them to a few local film historians).

After La Marr died, the Castle went through several different owners, all of whom had vastly different tastes. But rather than make sweeping changes across the entire villa, they made small, piece-meal alterations, such as adding new hardwood floors to only one of the hallways or bedrooms, without any thought as to whether it followed the same aesthetic as the rest of the house. There were at least five different types of wood flooring spread across the three levels. I wish I could watch a time-lapse video of all the people who'd lived in the Castle after La Marr, up to when we bought it.

There's an old saying: "Nobody is *from* Los Angeles. Everybody comes *to* Los Angeles." How many millions of people have made the pilgrimage to California to build a new life? That's what the Castle represented—a hodgepodge of different ideas, ambitions, histories, personalities (and design tastes!), all crammed together under the same roof and a boatload of turrets, across a slew of random wood floors. If the history of the house could be made visible, what a great Hollywood story it would make.

And then, like any Hollywood story, the producer would swoop in and fix it in editing. That was me! Our first day on the site, the first words out of my mouth were: "Tear it all out!"

We knew right away that we had to start knocking down walls and opening it up, but beyond that, we weren't sure. With some houses, it's obvious the moment you enter what to do, but with others, like this one, you have to walk the floors, slow down, pay attention. We had to walk through it a few times to make sense of it, to envision what we wanted it to become. To give us some direction, we had to picture the whole family living in it, friends visiting, dinner parties underway, holidays celebrated.

We wanted the first floor of the Castle to be more open, cozier, more welcoming. When a house has been chopped up into too many rooms and the walls make everything feel closed off and small, it's like the house itself is begging to breathe. Logically, you'd think having seven bedrooms is perfect for a big family like ours, but you know what's even better? A big, open space where everyone can see one another. We want to be with our kids, not have them retreating into small, separate rooms.

The kids had been hopeful that they would get their own bedroom at last in the seven-bedroom house. So when they realized we were knocking down walls, and the privacy they'd been anticipating wasn't going to happen, they protested. Making sure there was a music room so the boys could rock out (complete with DIY soundproofing) and a mini theater (a great asset when you resell a Hollywood Hills home) earned us some points.

Breaker and Wolfie shared a small bedroom on the main floor; Five, Holleder, and Major all shared a bedroom on the second floor; and the girls, Bellamy and Tallulah, had the lower floor as a bedroom. Despite their initial disappointment that they weren't all going to have their own fortresses of solitude, they saw the value in shared space, in being part of a collective where you couldn't hide away. I think that's what New York taught us: family connection doesn't flourish in an environment with more doors and opportunities for seclusion. When you're in each other's faces and you can't run away and slam a bedroom door to escape, you have to deal with everything—the good and the bad of being in a family. If you have the biggest house on the block, you should have the fewest number of walls. Then you get to fumble your way through the messy but eternally rewarding process of learning to share space, get along, and love each other through it.

During all our renovations, we have to fulfill the needs of our family while simultaneously keeping the future in mind, since we know we'll sell the place one day. We wanted this house to truly belong in the Hollywood Hills, like a boutique hotel with its own colorful past. Like you could walk in the front door and almost see Clark Gable and Carole Lombard sipping martinis in the corner. It was in this spirit that we tried to save as many of the original elements as we could, like the iron railing on the spiral staircase, installed by La Marr back in the roaring 1920s. (We added a contemporary pendant light to give the staircase a modern feel.) We also held on to the rotunda ceiling and the original front door, which had a fantastic peekaboo window.

As much as we loved the door, it was weirdly placed because it entered right into the kitchen, which just felt anticlimactic. You approach this grand house and walk inside to see…the oven? The entrance needed both more privacy and more drama. So we added a gated open-air vestibule, which offered just enough buffer before visitors reached the front entrance. It included a beautiful tiled landing that brought you to the front door, finished with blue and white vintage Moroccan tile and bougainvillea.

Unfortunately, much of the original interior could not be saved, like the old windows, a ragtag collection of too many different styles. So Cortney and Bellamy sold all of them, right out of our garage. We made a good amount of money, which went toward the purchase of custom steel windows made by a local manufacturer. They were extremely expensive, but we knew they would transform the home, and the money would come back to us when we one day sold the Castle.

The wood floors obviously had to go, too. We were creating a fresh canvas—new stucco, the steel windows, and gorgeous wood floors. We paid top dollar for reclaimed oak floors made by Schotten & Hansen, a Bavarian company, and never regretted it. When it comes to deciding where to put most of your budget, floors are never a bad idea, especially when you use a hardwood that just gets better with age.

Like we did in the Berkshires, we painted the main downstairs all white, which made the house feel whole, united. The bathrooms got major overhauls, too. One of the benefits of the branding partnerships we've maintained over the years is that we tend to get free stuff during renovations with the (correct) expectation that the products will get their due in magazine features and online profiles. Cortney was currently working with Toto, so all of our toilets were heated. Have you ever tried a heated seat first thing in the morning? It's pretty, pretty great. But nothing is free. Cortney had to sell toilets in Vegas, and on her return home, she told the kids, "It's a shitty business."

One thing that *lacked* sophistication was the clunky, inelegant gate and the wall that surrounded the property. We weren't thrilled with it, but we didn't have the budget to change the entire thing (and we weren't going to piecemeal it, as had been done with the floors). Even tearing it down would've been too costly. We either had to live with it or reimagine it.

We decided to give it a fresh paint job and throw black and white Sunbrella fabric over some sections to give it a Hollywood Regency look, a more engaging and visually interesting aesthetic. We also invested in hedges, which both disguised the wall and gave us an extra layer of privacy from street traffic. Now, instead of feeling like we lived in a prison, we were surrounded by beautiful shrubbery.

There are really no negatives in home renovation if you stay in an optimistic state of mind. I know it's cliché, but every problem really can be embraced as an opportunity. One of the most valuable skills you can develop as a home renovator applies to every other facet of life: if something can go wrong, it will (eventually). What matters is how you react. You can push for the outcome you wanted, digging in your heels and demanding that reality live up to expectations. Or you can adapt and change. Instead of obsessing over what you *can't* do, focus on what *can* be done.

It's also important to find a source of inspiration to guide your renovation, a place you can visit in person or virtually and return to when you need a lift, or a reminder of the atmosphere and energy you are designing toward, and how it will feel once you're done. This will keep you going, keep your creative fires burning.

We found our inspiration a few blocks away, at the Chateau Marmont. During our regular breakfasts there, Robert and I would revel in the atmosphere and brainstorm on the design of our new home. Our new, pristine white stucco, the pinstriped Sunbrella fabric around our metal gate, and the Moroccan tile at the entrance

"

There are really no
negatives in home
renovation if you stay
in an optimistic state of
mind. I know it's cliché,
but every problem
really can be embraced
as an opportunity.

Cortney taking a rest during construction

were all thanks to the Chateau Marmont breakfasts we enjoyed while soaking up the Chateau's Old World charm. Their designers seamlessly combined indoor and outdoor spaces, and their use of color and antiquities was masterful—not perfect, but perfect for us.

One of my favorite days in the Hills was when the moving trucks finally pulled up with all our belongings that had been in storage for more than a year. Living for that long in a rental, with not enough space and without your stuff, can start to wear you down. You miss your things, the furniture and art and photos that feel so much a part of your personal identity—and your family's identity.

The furniture brand Dedon gifted us an unbelievable collection of outdoor pieces, because they predicted the home would get a lot of press. It was a special day. The kids all ran outside to greet the trucks like it was Christmas. For the first time, it felt like we lived here. Not just at the Castle, but in Los Angeles, in California. We finally had an address that belonged to us. We weren't tourists anymore. We were *locals*.

We soon cherished our new home. I became a decent swimmer with daily dips in our saltwater pool. We explored and enjoyed the magnificent state of California: we hiked in the San Gabriel Mountains, took the boys to epic skate parks in Venice Beach, went on road trips

Breaker jumping into the pool

to Joshua Tree, went skiing in Big Bear, enjoyed beach days in Malibu. That was why we had come here! Reality TV was great—we're so grateful for those opportunities—but the experiences and memories I hold close are the ones that have nothing to do with celebrity and publicity, but with family, with never taking for granted that wherever we are, whatever we're doing, we're in it together.

I wanted to fall in love with Southern California, I really did. But it still felt like I was on vacation—meaning, far from home. Nothing about it seemed real. I was still focused on how different it was from New York, and resisted embracing what made life in LA special and unique.

So what turned me around?

Gardening.

The Castle's huge backyard offered more gardening real estate than I'd ever had back East. In New York, you have to make do with small rooftop gardens or whatever you can squeeze into window flower boxes. But here, the outdoor area was almost as expansive as the house itself. We could have left it as a big, grassy lawn, but that seemed like a waste. This kind of natural canvas calls for something beautiful and bold.

Robert got many of the amenities he'd been hoping for, like an outdoor fireplace and refrigerator and, of course, a pizza oven. We came to realize that living in Los Angeles means living outdoors more than in, and mornings and evenings are the best part. The new outdoor furniture made it comfortable. For the hot afternoons, we had an awning where we could find respite from the sometimes unrelenting sun. We cooked outside almost every night.

Eventually, I started to crave getting my hands dirty. I wanted my fingers in the soil. But I needed some guidance, so I started meeting with Victor, a landscape artist who lived and breathed local flora. This wonderful man became a gardening and landscaping mentor for me.

I'd gardened before, but not in a place like this. I knew almost nothing (nor did Robert), about how to garden in Southern California. Victor would pick me up every morning in his truck. One morning we drove more than two hours to look for the perfect trees. We picked out thirty in all: olive trees and citrus trees, which I gravitated toward not just for their color but for the fruit they provided. The thought of growing food in my own backyard was invigorating.

This became a spiritual journey for me. I always feel energized and inspired when immersed in a renovation project, but I was never quite able to shake my homesickness. As a mom, I was carrying the struggles of all of my kids as they navigated a new city. I missed the energy and excitement of Manhattan. I missed my friends. I missed walking and the spontaneous moments that happen only in New York. There is something to be said about building roots. But because my nature is to lean into the positive, instead of worrying about what I'd lost, I tuned in to where I was and what was all around me. I've always loved gardening, but this was different.

You don't need to make a place for nature in LA like you do in New York. You're in the *middle* of nature. Gardening, and then more and more hiking, helped me embrace the peace that came with being surrounded by so much bountiful plant life. Change is hard. But creating and then tending to a garden healed me in ways I didn't even realize I needed to be healed.

Wherever Robert and I may go in the future, however far we stray from home, it's a lesson that I hope will always stay with me: don't look at what your life *used* to be. Open your eyes and look around at where you live *now*.

Having fun with the decor

Robert and Cortney taking the plunge

9

NEVER (*EVER*) TAKE
YOUR EYE OFF THE BALL
Bird Streets House
Hollywood Hills, California

This isn't going to be an easy chapter for us to write. Because the Bird Streets house—from rehab to final sale—wasn't an easy chapter for us to live.

This was not a time when years of perfecting our design skills came to fruition, when time spent working as a duo in perfect tandem paid off, when our decisions about what to buy (and when) were gracefully executed, or when we stuck to our tried-and-true approach to guiding a renovation all the way through to an outstanding result.

The route to feeling like the bottom had fallen out was slightly circuitous, so stick with us, as the journey is important to share. It's a universal truth that messing up can teach us as much about ourselves and what to do better in the future as any smashing success (maybe more). It's not a fun truth, but it's our truth.

Ironically, the moment when everything came into question was also the moment we got one of our biggest paydays. Just a week after we'd listed the Castle, we received an offer—for *a million more* than the asking price. They hadn't even seen the place in person yet, just did a photo tour online. The catch—and it was a big one: they wanted us out in two weeks.

It's not like we hadn't moved in a hurry before—we know how to pack fast—but something about this move felt *too* fast, *too* hurried, *too* frantic, even though we know it's part of the deal, as this is the life, and the business, we've chosen. By the time we had to make the bionic move out of the Castle, we'd been living this way for almost twenty-five years. We put everything we have into a home, and for however long we live there, we make it our own. Then, whether it's years or months (or weeks!) into settling in, we sell it and say goodbye. We always know it's not going to be forever.

We couldn't exactly turn down the offer (nor did we want to at the time). We had debts, and this money would allow us to buy our next house debt-free for the first time. But we also weren't ready to make some of the huge decisions that were in front of us. We'd moved to California in 2014 with the agreement that we'd stay for two years max. Two years had turned into three, and then four. Now it was 2019, and we had no plan. Were we going to look for another house to over-haul in LA and keep building our business out West? Or were we heading back to New York City, as I'd promised Cortney would happen eventually?

We were at a major crossroads, and the deal was forcing our hand. Within a year we'd have three kids in private colleges, which, as you know, are not cheap. Concurrently, we'd also have the younger kids in private schools. It's not news that the expense is enormous.

A wise friend recently asked: What would you tell your younger self? I didn't have to think very hard or very long: I'd put my kids in public schools from start to finish. Cortney and I were both products of public school, so there was no real issue with it. In SoHo, however, there was a dearth of public schools, and middle schools in the city are notoriously not great. So it just turned out that way. We're grateful to the community of schools that nourished our kids, and none of us have a crystal ball or a time machine to travel back and do it differently.

We have to look ahead. Which in this case meant taking advantage of offers like this one on the Castle.

We got the offer on a Monday. We were hosting the wedding of dear friends on the following Saturday, and by the end of the next week, we had to be out of the Castle. We were already committed to the wedding and didn't want to stress our friends out, so we kept the news to ourselves. I was overwhelmed by the prospect of the money and all it would mean for us, but I was also utterly panicked. Robert and I were well aware of the rental housing market in LA and how hard it is to find something—even when you have time.

Underneath all of the overwhelm was a sense of real dismay. It had taken me so long—and so much soul-searching—to find my footing after the move to California, and to make the Castle feel like a true home, *our* home. The kids had finally hit their stride, and this was in large part due to having been in the house for almost four years—a long time for us. Although we had put the house on the market, selling it seemed far in the future, something we could prepare for emotionally and psychologically. But two weeks? I almost couldn't bear it.

We did end up finding a place to land while we figured out our next move (so to speak). It wasn't bad, given the rush we were in to secure something. Its location in West Hollywood worked well, as the kids could still walk everywhere, and most of all, it was available on short notice. (Incidentally, the previous tenants were pop-culture icon Kylie Jenner and rapper and record producer Travis Scott.) But—though it's a matter of opinion—some might say it was the beginning of the end for us in Los Angeles.

Once we moved in and were as settled as we could be, I started driving around, looking for our next project. We hadn't come to a clear understanding about what would come next, no explicit conclusions about whether we were staying or going, buying here or somewhere else. It was a fraught topic between me and Cortney. We'd try to talk about it, and then fight, then try again, then fight again. It was not an easy time.

Even so, at this point in our careers and family life, it was almost routine: sell, move, rent, hunt. So that's what I did. I hunted, without knowing exactly what we'd do if I found something. In hindsight, the decision to sell the Castle, though it would have seemed counterintuitive to turn down the offer, was a pretty bad strategic move on my part. Cortney's instincts were 100 percent accurate.

Our time in that house was the happiest of times—we've never loved a home more, and our family was flourishing. As a result of me pushing the sale, not only did I lose the Castle, but I ultimately lost Los Angeles, a city I'd grown to love. I felt I held the secret to making money, a kind of magic fairy dust—a formula that had always worked in the past. I could just keep re-creating it, couldn't I? But anytime you think you're bulletproof is the moment you're doomed to failure.

It was Cortney who would find our next place, by doing something almost nobody else does in Los Angeles: walking.

One thing I loved about LA was walking through the Hollywood Hills. I had one girlfriend who loved it, too, so we would walk first thing in the morning down Hollywood Boulevard and then south and over to Sunset and into the Bird Streets. We'd meander through the different neighborhoods and "decorate" houses while we walked, pointing out what we'd change, add, or take away from what we could see from the sidewalk. I didn't think of these walks, at least not consciously, as house hunting, but just as getting outside and moving my body.

One fateful morning, my friend and I ended up exploring the Bird Streets, the very fancy neighborhood above the Sunset Strip dating back to the early 1920s, full of TV and film stars' homes (we saw Jimmy Kimmel on the regular). For all you non-Californians, the area didn't get its name because of its bird population. The Bird

"

It was Cortney who
would find our next place,
by doing something
almost nobody else does
in Los Angeles: walking.

Streets are called that because of their avian names: Oriole Way, Skylark Lane, Nightingale Drive, Warbler Place, to name just a few. The most famous is certainly Blue Jay Way, where George Harrison, waiting for his publicist outside his rental house on that street, wrote the song with that name ("There's a fog upon LA, and my friends have lost their way," go the opening lyrics). It appeared on the Beatles' *Magical Mystery Tour* album. The Bird Streets area somehow manages to feel as refined and impeccable as Beverly Hills, which it borders, but with the laid-back, relaxed vibe of the Hollywood Hills. The best of both worlds—assuming you can afford it.

We'd fallen in love with a house in the Bird Streets neighborhood before, the aforementioned old Hollywood mansion owned by Mitzi Shore, cofounder and longtime owner of the Comedy Store. Her villa on Doheney, built in the 1920s and previously owned by Hollywood legend Dorothy Lamour, had been an after-party spot for the performers who came through the venue—Richard Pryor, Andrew Dice Clay, Robin Williams, and on and on. It was an impressive piece of property, with its Spanish tile roof and balconies overlooking West Hollywood. It looked like something you'd see in Provence. There was something about those old mansions in the Hills that captivated me—their ties to old Hollywood and the stories that lived in their bones, or the architecture that was hard to believe existed in any US city, or the era they were built in. Or all three, in some cases.

We'd missed our chance with Mitzi's classic Hollywood home— it was on the market in 2014, when we hadn't been in Los Angeles for long, so we were nervous about pulling the trigger. We kicked ourselves for a long time over that one, but we also knew that there's always another house around the corner.

The thing that really pains me, even to this day? Real-estate mogul Kurt Rappaport (who'd listed it) bought it himself for around $5 million and gave it a complete makeover, adding a gym, wine cellar, and sixty-foot pool. Based on the pictures I've seen, it looked like a

McMansion, with no reverence for the building's history. Our instincts were right—though we would have kept all the charm and modernized the home. In 2018, he sold it to Tinder founder Sean Rad for a jaw-dropping $26.5 million. C'est la vie.

I was excited to find out that we'd get another chance at a house in the Bird Streets.

During one of my Bird Streets walks, I stumbled upon a house for sale on Cordell Drive, just around the corner from Mitzi's—or, rather, Sean Rad's. As I started assessing it from a house-hunting perspective, I felt a growing dread. It had everything we look for: it was on a corner on an isolated stretch of road, with low traffic. It was high up, so there were views, yet still close enough to Sunset that you wouldn't be entirely trapped on the hill. And because it was in terrible shape (a plus for us), it was within our price range. Did I have to tell Robert?

Even after settling into the rental, I wasn't in the best shape emotionally. I was keeping up a brave face for my kids, but I was suffering. This was unlike me. We'd spent a lot of time between houses, waiting for move-in dates, waiting to sell, not selling as quickly as we'd like or at the price we would have liked, but I'd always felt resilient. This time, I wasn't bouncing back. Since that wonderful day at the Castle when our stuff arrived from the East Coast and we were finally able to move in, I'd felt so hopeful, like maybe we could do this—keep making a life in LA.

To say I was excited to have found the house in the Bird Streets would be a lie. I knew Robert would fall in love with it, and I couldn't handle the thought of undertaking another reno, here in this city I hadn't *really* wanted to come to in the first place.

I did fall in love with it, and I knew, just as Cortney knew, that it would be a *really* smart investment. It was in a wildly popular and sought-after neighborhood where home values were climbing every year. We weren't

above and opposite: Before the demolition

ahead of the curve on this one like we had been with the neighborhoods we'd bought into in New York—this was already one of the hot-
test high-end neighborhoods in LA. But it was an extraordinarily safe
bet. If we played our cards right, we'd be able to sell it for a huge profit
and use the money to fund our next project.

But there was a big problem. Cortney didn't want to live there.

**From afar, the house on Cordell seemed intriguing enough. But
when I finally got inside, it left me cold. I don't know another way**

to say it. I couldn't imagine creating memories there—whether it was hosting friends and laughing into the night while playing family games or just cozying up in front of the TV with family. Nothing about it called out to me, made me want to lay down roots.

Whether you're designing a home you hope to live in for a long time or plan to sell to the highest bidder someday, if you don't get butterflies in your stomach every time you visit the worksite, it will show in your work. You risk the house looking like a spec home. And a spec home isn't made from love; it's made for profit. But

"

The homes that I'm proudest of, that I think truly represent what Robert and I do best, we built for ourselves.

that's ultimately what this house would be—a house we rebuilt to sell to someone else.

The homes that I'm proudest of, that I think truly represent what Robert and I do best, we built for ourselves. We didn't build them for investors, or brokers, or some crazy dream of hitting the real estate jackpot. We built them with the idea that someday, Robert and I might be sitting on rocking chairs on the front porch, holding hands and waiting for our grandkids to show up.

Robert was of course disappointed when I told him how I felt. He was sure that if we did our magic, gave it some "tender loving care," I might feel differently. I tried to find a way to explain that I couldn't even imagine *wanting* to do that. He was so full of joy and optimism, and all I could see was a dark cloud moving in over us. I knew no good could come from hiding it, so I had to tell him the things nobody wants to say to a partner, and that no partner wants to hear: "I'm not happy." I missed our life in New York. I loved him, but I didn't love this. "I can't do this anymore." Not here, I told him.

The busier our lives had become with driving to and from various obligations, the less contact I had with actual people. I spent more time in carpool lanes than talking to other adults face-to-face. I missed the Manhattan days of walking to school for pickup or sitting with other parents on park benches while our children played in the park. Instead, I was waving to other parents from my car. That experience of connection had disappeared. I was lonely and ready to go home.

My desire to stay in California was multilayered. First and foremost, staying made so much more sense to me than going back to Manhattan, and I simply felt like it was best for our family. It was a no-brainer financially. New York's cost of living was twice that of LA's, taxes were much higher there, and we had a big group of people to move around, so it was a lot to navigate.

It's also true that I loved Los Angeles. I loved going to see my favorite bands on a weekly basis at the Hollywood Bowl and the Greek Theater, watching my beloved Dodgers play at Chavez Ravine, eating the famous chicken parmesan at the outstanding Dan Tana's on Santa Monica Boulevard in West Hollywood. I loved that in a single day we could drive from the Stahl House in West Hollywood (a masterpiece of mid-century modern architecture) to the Eames House in Pacific Palisades (created in 1949 by our heroes, the design duo Charles and Ray Eames), to the Greystone Mansion in Beverly Hills (a Tudor-style estate by Hoover Dam architect Gordon Kaufmann), to the Lummis House, aka El Alisal, on the edge of Arroyo Seco (a castle hand-built from stones in the late nineteenth and early twentieth centuries).

Cortney and Major and I loved walking the iconic Rose Bowl Flea Market and the Long Beach Antique Market. And I'd take Major to the skate park in Venice Beach. I loved walking to the Los Angeles County Museum of Art. I loved hiking all over LA—in Franklin Canyon Park and in Fryman Canyon off Mulholland Drive—and visiting the beaches up and down the Southern California coast. I am reminded of the quote (often misattributed to novelist Kurt Vonnegut but in actuality published by *Chicago Tribune* columnist Mary Schmich) that you should "live in New York City once, but leave before it makes you hard," and live in California once, too, "but leave before it makes you soft." So, yeah, I loved Los Angeles—can you tell? I wasn't ready to return to the hardness and concrete.

Fortunately, Robert didn't argue that I should love LA like he did. He brought it back to the big picture. "New York isn't going anywhere," he told me. "And if we don't give this an honest shot, we might regret it someday. It's not like we're going to come back here again in twenty years for another try."

So we compromised: we would buy the house on Cordell, we'd work fast like we tend to do anyway, and once it was finished, we'd move back to New York. No exceptions. I felt better knowing she trusted me, and I think she felt better knowing I was serious about this not being forever.

There was no way around the reality: I loved LA and liked New York. Cortney loved New York and hated LA.

George Cukor, the legendary Oscar-winning Hollywood film-maker was, like Cortney and me, an old-time New Yorker with the East Coast in his blood, who, like me, also loved California. He was once quoted in *Architectural Digest*: "It bothers me when people dis-parage Los Angeles. They say that they miss the culture of New York and that New York is so stimulating. Well, I say if you're not dull your-self, you'll find it just as stimulating here."

Everything about that rings true for me. Not that I think Cortney is dull—of course not!—but just that my experience was that LA is what you make it. It's a different world from New York, and you can't make it be what it isn't. Once you start comparing them, you're not being fair. It's like telling a great friend you wish they could be like your other great friend. Los Angeles is exactly what it should be. It has its own rhythms, its own advantages and disadvantages, its own secret corners and hidden gems for those willing to find them.

Coincidentally, Cukor's home—or at least the home he lived in until his death in 1983—was *right across the street* from the house we were buying. We were transplanted New Yorkers, living in the shadow of Cukor, the patron saint of New Yorkers trying to find the beauty in this foreign land called California. Talk about *kismet*!

Kismet was the last thing on Cortney's mind, but as much as I could hear in her voice how desperately she wanted to go back to New York ASAP, where she felt like she was home, she could hear in mine that I needed to do this, that I wasn't done with Los Angeles.

As much as Robert was trying to persuade me, it wasn't working. Still, we had to have a party. Our construction parties always gave us good mojo, so we had one on Cordell. It did feel great to bring some energy to the place. We striped the emptied-out pool pink

and white, and our son Breaker and his band played in there. We even hired a small group of dancers from the Los Angeles Ballet, who came in their tutus and pointe shoes. Kids and grown-ups alike christened the walls with chalk and paint—walls that would be getting demoed to nothing in a matter of weeks.

I admit, it was a blast.

As fun as the party was, I knew the party in the bigger sense, the LA party, was over unless I could pull off some eleventh-hour miracle, as Cortney had one foot out the door. It was time to get down to business. And the house was clearly going to require more than a few coats of paint and new furniture. Not a full teardown, but definitely a gut job.

We hired the architect we used for the Castle, who coincidentally also had done the Mitzi Shore house around the corner, which gave us a lot of confidence that we had a winner on our hands. We also used the same general contractor we'd worked really well with on the Castle. So we felt like we had a great team assembled—though we'd come to discover that they had ideas we weren't fully on board with. The house wasn't structurally sound, they said, and they wanted to tear it down.

By the summer of that year, we started hitting major delays with the build. In addition to the disagreement with our contractor, there were new building regulations and permit issues that had not existed when we'd rehabbed the Castle. So things were moving very slowly. I knew I wasn't going to last.

"I want to go home," I told Robert, and, thinking practically, it needed to be soon, so the kids could start the school year where they could also finish it. We could finish the house, I suggested, from New York. We'll commute.

I can't say I was surprised, but I was definitely disappointed. As Murphy's Law goes, everything that can go wrong will. The delays only soured Cortney that much more on the house…and on Los Angeles.

Cortney had stayed well past our initial agreement, and though I'd hoped she'd have a change of heart about California, she had given it a real chance. I now had to show her the same consideration when she hit tilt on the West Coast. Marriage is about sacrifice, and it cuts both ways.

We moved back to New York City in late summer to get the kids started in school, believing we'd left the Bird Streets house in the hands of a team we could trust enough to build while we were on the other side of the country. It would be no small task, especially with the foundation being on a hillside. The terrain on the hills there can be very tricky.

Within a few weeks, I commuted back to LA, arriving at the site to see that most of the house had been torn down, which I wasn't at all expecting. My dream house had become a bad dream—and for the first time I wasn't sure what to do. The architect told me it was actually good news: we could now build a much bigger and better house from scratch. Plus a full rebuild in LA is worth a lot more than a renovation, as you are essentially selling a brand-new, perfectly built house. It made a lot of sense, and I slept a little bit better that night, though the general contractor and I were still not in agreement on how to move forward.

I interviewed a few new general contractors I'd never worked with. They had done great work, yet were more expensive than what I was used to. The one I ended up hiring was confident he would keep everything at budget or below—which, of course, did not end up being the case. We had to shut down for a month or so to get permits transferred to the new contractor. In that time, we hired a talented designer to take over in Cortney's absence on-site. Finally, around the holidays, we got going. We had our team in place and were rolling.

But of course that was not the end of the Age of Obstacles. Did we mention that this was the holidays of 2019? So you know what came next: March 2020 and the COVID-19 pandemic.

Though things had not gone to plan and were still not going to plan, I've never lost sight of the fact that we work best as a team. We always

have. And not just because we naturally get along. When we take on a new project, it's not a side hustle. It's not "we'll get to it when we have time." It becomes all-consuming. When we're not on the job site, we're thinking about the job site. When we're sleeping, we're usually dreaming about the job site. We become like a two-headed hydra. Robert notices details I would've missed, because I'm so laser-focused on some other aspect of the renovation, and vice versa. This is a rare thing that we have as a couple. So I didn't blame him for how things were unfolding, and I did my best to do my part from New York while he was commuting and trying to iron out the issues at the site on Cordell.

We now had a strong team, with the new general contractor and a top designer with fresh eyes, yet things were still not going smoothly. It wasn't just the first contractor tearing down the entire house while we weren't paying attention. The new one went ahead and took down all the beautiful trees. And while the new designer was doing a great job, money was no object, or it wasn't *her* object.

It was our own fault for looking away.

We tried to make the best of an unfortunate situation. With the house taken to the studs, we had to let go of some of our original vision and plan and try and build something new that felt special and exciting to us. We followed the general layout of the original house but made the ceilings taller, added another level, and made the courtyard our focal point. Making the bottom-floor ceilings higher and enlarging the window openings let in more light. The white oak floors and white walls gave it a modern but classic aesthetic. We hired the top millworker in Los Angeles to create gorgeous cabinetry and woodwork throughout the home. The exterior had a reclaimed terra-cotta roof with a white stucco facade. But the crème de la crème was the interior courtyard with its stunning tile and open sky, something we always dreamed of.

The new designer had managed to find the most expensive version of everything on our wish list, which put us perilously close to burning through our budget well before the finish line. She wasn't the same type of project manager that Cortney is. Her experience was more in design, not construction, and her taste was different than ours. And when it's your own money, you look at things differently.

We ended up building a beautiful house, and she was a part of that. Unfortunately, it felt like a lot of modern houses in the area, lacking the unique soul of the Castle and most of our other projects. We always say, "Once you're like everyone else, then you're like everyone else." We've historically received higher-than-market prices—our use of color, quirkiness, and fun is what people bought into.

Obviously, being a great house renovator isn't just about delegating. You need a team that understands your vision and shares your passion. But there's only so much they can do if you're not there. The moment you don't show up and assume that somebody else will get it right, do it how you would do it, that's when it's all going to fall apart.

We finally finished the house in late fall of 2020, and the timing could not have been more perfect. We hired the team Branden and Rayni Williams, superstar realtors of the Bird Streets. They loved the house and had offers within the first day.

Unfortunately, those offers were 20 percent less than what we thought the house was worth—and we passed. The Williamses were adamant that the offers were sound and in line with the market, and that we'd be lucky to get the very high asking price we'd put on the house.

Our luck was not yet ready to turn in a good direction. Within sixty days of the house being on the market, interest rates starting soaring higher and higher. *And* Los Angeles voted to enact a "mansion tax"—Measure ULA—requiring buyers to pay an additional 5.5 percent tax on home purchases over $5.5 million. This new measure literally stopped all sales of expensive homes in the Bird Streets. Pretty much overnight, there were no buyers.

The interior courtyard became the highlight of the renovation.

Robert and Cortney poolside

Then in early 2023, the US actors' union began what would turn out to be the biggest strike in the history of Hollywood, which certainly didn't help. As we did with 400 West, we learned the hard way, eventually selling the house for 20 percent less than the offers we'd had through the Williamses.

As bad as some of the decisions we made were, and how bad our luck was timing-wise, we still ended up making a little money, but not nearly enough to compensate for the stress it put on both of us. We also realized that we do best when we build for ourselves and are working as a team. We are not general contractors or spec builders. We're Bob and Cortney—and we're at our best when we work that way, together. For a stretch of time there, we forgot that. When we're on-site every day, watching every nail get hammered in, directing the construction like symphony conductors, that's when something special happens. Some jobs in this world you can phone in, but this absolutely isn't one of them.

A Waverly Place gem near Washington Square Park

10

THE PINK HOUSE
114 Waverly Place
Greenwich Village, New York

Rewind the timeline for a moment to the year-end holidays, 2018. I was still living in LA but dreaming of coming back to New York for good, and was there for a visit when I finally got a chance to peek inside one of my favorite New York buildings. The Pink House, as it was affectionately called thanks to its hard-to-miss bubblegum-pink facade, was a townhouse on Waverly Place, a block from Washington Square Park. Most folks in Manhattan knew the house, though almost nobody had actually crossed its threshold. And everybody was more than familiar with the owner, who was something of a local legend.

Celeste Martin, a former Rockette and actress, had lived in the Pink House for most of her life, having inherited it when her father passed away in the mid-1980s. Edmond, a French immigrant, had bought the building and five others in the neighborhood in the 1920s, renting them out to struggling artists for almost nothing. He was apparently the inspiration for the landlord character in the 1953 Broadway musical *Wonderful Town* (with music composed by

Leonard Bernstein) about two sisters with theater aspirations living in a Greenwich Village basement apartment.

Celeste had a life as colorful and eccentric as anything she played onstage. She was a fixture during Pride celebrations, watching the parade from her third-floor balcony, waving and blowing kisses to the people below. Even into her nineties, she always wore the same outfit: a tight-fitting halter top, short shorts, and a blonde wig. During her last decades, she lived mostly with her cats—the estimate stands at about thirty. Her feline roommates had the run of the place, inhabiting all four floors while Celeste kept to her chambers.

When the broker turned the key at the Pink House's front door and stepped aside to let me and my son Five enter, my first impression was a mix of excitement and uneasiness. To be sure, it was beautiful, with high ceilings and Beaux Arts–style architecture dating back to 1826—there had been, amazingly, only three owners since that early nineteenth-century date. But it was in a state of tragic disrepair, with holes in the walls and old boxes piled in every corner (Celeste was something of a hoarder). There were water stains everywhere from what the broker told me were likely burst pipes. And that was just the damage I noticed on a first quick walk-through. Hard to tell what we might find once we dug deeper.

"It's interesting that I'm showing you this place today of all days," the broker said.

"Why's that?"

He told me that Celeste had passed away that very morning. "She was ninety-eight years old," he said. "Or at least that's what her neighbors ballparked. Nobody really knows for sure. She definitely lived one hell of a life."

Her health had declined enough in recent months that she'd decided to put the house on the market, or at least put out feelers to prospective buyers. Robert was back in LA, working hard on the Bird Streets house—and I jumped at the chance for a private tour of a house I must've passed hundreds of times over the years.

Facade deterioration before the renovation

It was a four-story walk-up in New York with a *ballroom*. I mean, seriously? A grand ballroom with soaring twenty-two-foot ceilings and a massive arched window? I'd never seen anything like it before—not just in New York City, but anywhere.

Someone else looking around this place might mistakenly think it was one more burst pipe away from being condemned. But I could almost see what it had once been—a place of celebration. Celeste loved socializing with artists, the broker told me, and Five, fifteen at the time, also sensed this invisible history. Like most of his

Cortney and Robert in the cleared-out ballroom

"

It was the kind of magic
I always hope for when I
walk into a new building.
I would've liked it better
if the walls seemed less
on the verge of collapsing,
but the good energy was
undeniable.

siblings, he was getting tired of constantly moving and was unexcited by another walk-through of yet another house, but he moved through this one like he'd been here before, sure of where he was going, visibly relaxed and at ease, almost amused. I felt the same.

It was the kind of magic I always hope for when I walk into a new building. I would've liked it better if the walls seemed less on the verge of collapsing, but the good energy was undeniable. I thought of Celeste: Was she sizing me up the same way I was sizing up her house, trying to decide if I was a worthy owner? Just the thought gave me hope that this was somehow predestined.

Upstairs, the broker explained that at least two renowned artists had used the top-floor ballroom as a studio at different times. I gazed around in wonder at the incredible space. I could immediately envision our sons Breaker and Holleder playing piano, perhaps Breaker even composing a new song. Yes, I thought, *this* is what this house needs to become: a place for creative energy, for bringing new ideas to life, for gathering with friends and artists. And we could bring it into the future, give it the architectural facelift it so desperately needed.

I told the broker we were seriously interested, but that I had to talk to Robert.

The Pink House definitely exceeded our budget, but it was such a valuable piece of property that, given the asking price and recent sales in the area, its purchase seemed like a no-brainer. On the other hand, we were at this point just starting the Bird Streets house, after months of delays. If we bought this place, it would mean we'd be taking on the two biggest projects of our careers at the same time, one on each coast, which you could say more than stretched us—and stressed us. But being stretched and stressed never stopped us before. I felt confident we could do both projects and that Waverly could be a boon for us—it would push us as designers and give us the opportunity to do things we'd never done at this scale.

I've been a fan of the Village for a while, specifically that house. The pink facade was part of it, of course, but the whole history of the building is fascinating. It was originally built for Thomas Mercein, a former city comptroller and finance insurance company president. It was one of nine four-story houses built on that same street for Mercein, who apparently really liked to spread out. (Cortney and I have built all over the country, so I understand owning multiple homes, but almost a dozen houses on one block—is it excessive? Or impressive? I can't decide.)

114 Waverly, before it became the Pink House, got its first major design overhaul in 1920, when its new owner, architect William Sanger (his wife, Margaret Sanger, founded Planned Parenthood), gave it a curved roofline as well as round-arched windows and doorways in the art nouveau style.

The entire block had long been an oasis for artists and radical thinkers. The house next door, at 116 Waverly, was owned by painter and sculptor Anne Charlotte Lynch, who hosted a literary salon there on Saturday evenings that attracted some of the biggest writing talents of the time—Washington Irving, Herman Melville, William Cullen Bryant, Fitz-Greene Halleck, Margaret Fuller. At one gathering there in July 1845, Edgar Allan Poe gave the very first public reading of his soon-to-be-canonical poem "The Raven."

Right next door, more than a century later, Celeste Martin was doing her part to support the arts. Not just at the Pink House, but also at five other townhouses in the Village she'd inherited from her dad. She wasn't the best landlord when it came to repairs—many tenants claimed that their apartments were rat infested and in major disrepair—but she was kind, letting many of her tenants stay almost rent free. As one admirer tweeted on social media not long after Celeste's death, she "created a magical oasis for wayward artists and all-around misfits. We were safe in our two-hundred-year-old homes that tilted gently from the constantly rumbling subway and weight of the abundant wisteria vines."

The rooms needed to be emptied before the renovation could begin.

As her health began declining and bills were piling up even higher than usual, she decided to sell all her properties, including the Pink House. Maybe we just got lucky, or maybe Cortney was right and Celeste's spirit was still somewhere in those walls, the queen of the neighborhood giving us her blessing.

On August 9, 2019, we officially became the new owners of the Pink House on Waverly Place.

The house had history in its bones, and its original floor plan was solid: four floors, with room on the roof for a terrace and more than enough square footage for everything we needed. We've seen developers take a beautiful old house and transform it into a mega-mansion, adding floor upon floor, extravagance upon extravagance, until it starts to read more like a department store than a home. We weren't going to do that, and we thankfully wouldn't need to redesign the structure.

Yet once we officially owned the building and started assessing, it was in even worse shape than we'd thought, so more work than we'd anticipated. All that was salvageable were the original beams. Even the walls that could be spared needed extensive work.

A rehab is akin to open-heart surgery on a house. You crack open that rib cage not knowing what you're going to find inside. We often find surprises, and not always bad ones. In this case, we discovered gorgeous vintage wallpaper that had been hidden for decades behind layers of newer wallpaper and paint, and used its patterns to inspire our own Waverly collection with the Shade Store, which has become a very successful collection that we're very proud of. This is one of the ways we were able to bring echoes of the past into the future—both into our house and into the world.

We didn't want to create an exact duplicate of the house in the 1910s and 1920s, but we wanted hints of it, snapshots of a bygone era. Our general contractor, Gary, had been doing Manhattan projects with us for twenty years, and we had 100 percent confidence in

Bathroom before renovation

New bathroom with Gucci wallpaper

"

A rehab is akin to open-
heart surgery on a house.
You crack open that
rib cage not knowing what
you're going to find inside.
We often find surprises,
and not always bad ones.

him and his team. He was extremely safe and competent, and always did things by the book. He handled all of the construction aspects so Robert and I could focus on design and decor. We wanted the biggest renovation we'd done so far to be a major update but also to return the house to its former glory.

Though things were running smoothly, with Robert traveling to LA to oversee the Bird Streets house, we were running on all cylinders. And then New York, and most everywhere else, shut down.

It was scary when COVID-19 hit, but we'd watched a commercial airliner fly into the World Trade Center blocks from our home, and water from the Hudson River inch ever closer to our front steps, unsure when (or if) it would stop. We knew we'd get through this as a family. We'd stick close together like we always do. Like the rest of the world, we hoped for the best, and during the worst of it, when the streets in New York emptied, when the lines outside of hospitals grew, when the deaths from the virus rose and rose, we were able to hunker down at our Berkshires house—we were blessed—until it seemed like the absolute worst had passed and we returned to the city and our rental a few blocks from Waverly.

But when we got back, New York was still a ghost town and the Waverly Place project had come to a complete halt, pandemic restrictions having stopped construction on all nonessential sites, which included single-family homes. The fear and stress, stretched over many weeks, evolved into a restless urge to get back to work. When the city gave us the green light to return after a three-month stasis, the Department of Buildings had regular inspection sweeps for COVID-19 compliance. The site itself was subject to regulations—face masks, hygiene stations, warning signage, and more. We were limited to a specific maximum number of workers at the house at a given time. From a public-health standpoint, it made total sense. From a construction standpoint, it presented unique challenges. There were entire walls that needed erecting.

Things weren't so great in LA either; COVID-19 was everywhere. Yet Los Angeles, unlike New York, never put a complete halt on construction. We took a couple of weeks off to get the site ready (water and hygiene stations, proper signage). Our contractor in LA was diligent about following COVID guidelines, which we appreciated. These unavoidable delays, however, were costing us a lot of money and momentum. Time is money, and in construction, momentum is everything.

We also lost a lot of days due to supply-chain issues. It took an extra six months in some cases to get materials that were coming from all different parts of the country and world. For example, we might have all the materials we needed for new windows *except* the key hardware, which would then take four to five months to finally get to us. Things were definitely picking up, but some things took more time and cost more money.

We finally finished the Bird Streets house in the fall of 2021, after which I was back in New York full-time.

The one thing we didn't think would be an issue with the Pink House was the pink it was known for. The pink facade was what made the house so iconic, the first thing anybody mentioned when we told them about our latest project. "Oh, you bought the *Pink* House? I love that place!"

It was clear that the whole neighborhood and New York in general had a love affair with the house. So who would want to stop us from giving the building a fresh coat of pink paint? Well, the city's Landmarks Preservation Commission, that's who. Yes, Waverly was landmarked, and we'd committed the cardinal sin of buying a landmarked building. We'd heard it could take years sometimes to get approvals. Essentially, the commission needs to approve everything about the front of the house, including exterior lights, windows, railings, balconies, and any signage. For the most part, nobody cares what you do inside, but you need permits to change anything

about a building's external appearance. We went into this knowing we weren't going to fight the commission, as we had no interest in years of delays. Now, here's the thing: we didn't actually want to change anything at all. We just wanted to give the building a fresh coat of paint. It'd been sixty years since the house had gone pink, and the color's youthful pizzazz had faded over time. We loved the pink. But the commission had other ideas.

According to their guidelines, any paint job must be "consistent with the age and style of the building." That's exactly what we thought we were doing, but they wanted to be sure. So they required us to do a pigment test, which is where they take a paint sample and do optical microscopy to determine the exact color of a home when it was originally built. (In our case, that was two centuries ago.) It cost us $10,000 and the results were…inconclusive.

We made our arguments for pink, sharing the hundreds of articles about the property dating back to the 1970s that referred to it as the Pink House. But the commission wasn't interested. After weeks of debating, they came back and told us we had permission to use a brownstone stucco color that would blend in with the reddish-brown sandstone common in a lot of mid-nineteenth-century New York homes. Fine, we said. It wasn't our first choice by any means, but it wasn't worth the battle.

But when word got out, the commission was overrun with our Village neighbors protesting the decision, demanding that the Pink House remain pink. The commission agreed to "give it another review." We knew what this meant. We were in for endless delays while they tried to come to a consensus.

The commission members are all well-intentioned people who truly care about New York's historic buildings, and they were very nice to us. But their red tape is very red, and involves a lot of heated emotions around what "protecting history" means. With a house like ours, should we be protecting the home so it remains as close as possible to

Family portrait before renovation began in earnest

the building that members of the community recognize? Or do we transform it into what it might have looked like well before that, in the nineteenth century?

After a couple of confusing and inconclusive back-and-forths with the Landmarks Preservation Commission, then with the community board, then back to Landmarks, we waved the white flag. "We'll paint it any color you want," we said. "We'll paint it purple—just let us know." They finally came back with a color: a golden ocher. Overall, it seemed like the neighborhood was good with it, though we still get some snarky remarks about the absence of pink. We've learned over the years that you can't please everybody, especially New Yorkers.

Renovating a landmark can also be exhilarating. The new ocher color—what one journalist called "a bright warm yellow that shines like a sunflower"—really brightened up the block. And the entire community was eager to welcome us and share stories about Celeste. It seemed like everybody in the Village had tales about her—the parties and poetry readings, how much care she took with the people she loved, from friends and tenants to artists she barely knew.

We realized quickly that the Pink House was the highest-profile project we'd ever done—color, size, historical significance, location—so there were a lot of eyeballs on us, which can be fun but also a big headache. We've been doing this a long time, and so maybe we're showing our age, but it does feel like it used to be so easy. Well, not *easy*, but easi*er*. Everything has gotten more difficult, from inflation to property taxes to supply-chain issues to a chaotic building department, which has made renovating a townhouse that much harder.

When we were younger and nobody knew our names, we were easier to ignore. Probably because we just looked like two kids doing the best we could to build a home for our family. Now we live in a world of Google, Instagram, TikTok, and it's hard to stay low profile. Having what would turn into a popular reality show

didn't help the matter. There's an assumption that if you can afford a private home in Manhattan, you must be fabulously wealthy. That's never been the case with us. Every project, from the beginning in Chelsea to the Pink House, was done on a tight budget. It's why we buy furniture off the showroom floor and hunt for antiques rather than buying new. It's how we developed our eclectic style. A snarky reporter once said we were extremely lucky, and we agreed that luck had a lot to do with our success, but that reporter had no idea what it took to build in New York City. As Bette Davis might say, it ain't for sissies.

Once Gary's teams had completed a lot of the construction, Robert and I could focus on our role in this project—the interior. We rebuilt with materials that we hoped would last at least a few generations, which also honored the past of Waverly Place: Venetian plaster, German reclaimed-wood flooring, millwork, and windows, made by the finest craftspeople we could find.

We knew our future buyer would be a very wealthy individual who expected all the finishes to be incredible. What we've encountered in the past is that this type of serious buyer usually shows up with an entourage (architects, designers, contractors, and other people with opinions), and if things aren't perfectly built, with A+ finishes, you're going to hear about it—even if you've spent almost two years making the house perfect enough to make the cover of *House Beautiful* magazine, as was the case with Waverly Place. And they will still make changes. It's the nature of the beast.

We equipped the rooftop terrace with an entertainment lounge, a barbecue, and, of course, a pizza oven. We also spent quite a bit of time designing and decorating the ballroom, which spans 650 square feet and is accented by those 22-foot-high ceilings and a huge, arched window overlooking Waverly Place. We knew that Celeste hosted regular poetry readings in the space, and painter and muralist Jacob Getlar Smith used it as a studio during the 1940s, as did another artist or two after that. We knew we wanted the space to be

The magnificent ballroom reimagined

multifunctional, big enough to host several hundred people—for dinner parties with live musical entertainment, or special occasions such as our daughter Bellamy's engagement party, or performances by our son Breaker and his band.

The room also definitely called for big art, so big it wouldn't fit in the eight-person elevator or around the corners of the staircase. So our team had to use hand cranes to lift the huge art pieces up four stories and in through the massive window. The real doozy was getting a Steinway baby grand piano up to the ballroom, which we thought would be impossible, or craned through the window, which would cost almost as much as the piano itself.

We were wrong. The Steinway team showed up a week ahead to survey and measure our staircase. They said they could do it, which shocked us. But what really blew our minds was how they got it up the stairs. The Steinway truck pulled up in front of the house, and four men built like football players emerged, pulling out the piano. It had been disassembled into three or four pieces, the body separated from the legs. The men secured heavy-duty moving blankets onto the stairs with duct tape, then proceeded to wrap the body of the piano in additional blankets. They then *pushed* the piano—estimated somewhere between six and eight hundred pounds—up the stairs. Within an hour it was assembled and being tuned. Then the team supervisor instructed me to inspect the stairs to confirm there was nary a scratch. I told him I was more impressed that our stairs even held the weight, including the four men, which had probably totaled close to two thousand pounds.

Once we got the piano up, we knew we needed an amazing fireplace for the room's centerpiece. We found a reclaimed fireplace mantel at our go-to architectural artifact store, Olde Good Things. We debated the color for more than a year. I thought a dark blue would be more classic, but Robert had fallen in love with the Gucci store on West Broadway in SoHo—not with the clothes but with the colors of the interior. He did some investigating to identify the exact

"

The last thing we did is
what I'm probably most
proud of with this house:
I hired two friends from
the Berkshires to help
me landscape and build
a garden. This was the most
fun I had with anything
in the house—from start
to finish.

gold-yellow he was so taken with (some employees thought he was casing the store because he kept going in and not buying anything). We also ended up with some of Gucci's marvelous, fabulous wallpaper throughout the house. We tend to find design inspiration from boutique hotels, restaurants, and tasteful retail shops.

The last thing we did is what I'm probably most proud of with this house: I hired two friends from the Berkshires to help me landscape and build a garden. This was the most fun I had with anything in the house—from start to finish. The three of us went on a botanical expedition, starting with four dogwood trees we found at a Berkshires nursery, then visited every nursery north of New York, laughing and debating the best combination of shrubs, flowers, and ivies. Back at Waverly Place, we discovered a dirt pit on the roof that we converted into the garden. I still had the gardening bug from gardening in Los Angeles, so I was more excited than ever to see what I could do.

In the past, the majority of our renovation budget went to interiors—bathrooms are a bigger priority than flowers—but this time, with the roof such an ideal setting for a terrace, we built it into the budget so I didn't have to wait and see what was left when the final nails went in. I was planting even before some of the walls went up. So by the time the house was finished, the garden had a year of growth and was on its way to maturity. My friends from the Berkshires were great at making the venture economical—we planted a virtual jungle for a fraction of what landscapers would cost in the city—but the real joy was in the collaborating.

In many ways, the Waverly project felt like a full-circle moment for us. The first property Robert and I renovated together, in Chelsea, was less than a mile away. And just like that place, our new house had a yellow facade and spectacular views of the Empire State Building. It's staggering to think that was almost thirty years ago. We've come so far since then, and from a purely geographical standpoint, we've barely left.

Will this one be forever? Every time, I want to say yes. But it doesn't matter how much I love a home, or how grateful I am for everything we've built; it's only a matter of time before I get the itch. Before we *both* get it. I can't see a time when we're *not* hunting for the next design adventure, seeing what we can create from nothing. It can be exhausting, for sure, especially as we get older, and it's scary to move, to live in that uncertainty that hangs over us when we aren't sure if things are going to work out. Deep down, though, I know there'd be no shame in staying in this amazing house.

Maybe it will be our forever house… and maybe it won't.

The rooftop view

Acknowledgments

Many individuals fueled the creation of this book. It all started with our remarkable agent, Ian Kleinert, whose unwavering belief in our vision kick-started the project. We owe a great deal of gratitude to our exceptional editor, Jennifer Thompson, whose invaluable contributions took the book to new heights. We also want to express appreciation for Eric Spitznagel, whose insights and wit enriched the endeavor. We can't forget Laura Didyk, whose infectious enthusiasm and guidance lifted our spirits throughout. And last but not least, we're deeply thankful to the talented photographers we've had the privilege of collaborating with for nearly three decades: Gus Black, Ariadna Buffi, Tim Geaney, Catherine Hall, Nathan Johnson, Dean Kaufman, Kyle Knodell, Luc Roymans, Staci Marengo, Joshua McHugh, Costas Picadas, Amy Neunsinger, William Waldron, Mathew Williams, and many more.

About the Authors

Cortney and Robert Novogratz met in Charlotte, North Carolina, in June 1992, and soon after, they headed to New York City together. By 1996, they were married and had settled into their first Manhattan home. Over the years, they've built a diverse portfolio, designing residences across the globe. Their work caters to both celebrities and everyday clients, and they often collaborate with brands like Old Navy, Microsoft, and Procter & Gamble.

Their television career includes shows on Bravo and HGTV, alongside the publication of five books. They've been featured in various media outlets, including *Today* and *Good Morning America*, and recently appeared on the cover of *House Beautiful* magazine.

Outside of media, they've developed a furniture and home brand with a focus on accessible design. Their products are now available nationwide and in the UK. Amid their professional endeavors, they've raised a family of seven children and their much-adored dog, Winter. Despite their wide-reaching work, they remain connected to their home city of New York.

PUBLISHED BY
Princeton Architectural Press
A division of Chronicle Books LLC
70 West 36th Street, New York, NY 10018
papress.com

EDITOR: Jennifer N. Thompson
DESIGNER: Paul Wagner

LIBRARY OF CONGRESS CATALOGING-IN-PUBLICATION DATA
Names: Novogratz, Cortney, author. | Novogratz, Robert, author.
Title: The Novogratz chronicles : lessons learned from twenty-five years of
    buying and renovating houses / Robert Novogratz, Cortney Novogratz.
Description: First edition. | New York : Princeton Architectural Press, [2024] |
    Summary: "Robert and Cortney Novogratz share their trade secrets
    and personal stories from over twenty-five years of buying, selling, and
    fixing spaces and homes" —Provided by publisher.
Identifiers: LCCN 2024010099 | ISBN 9781797228624 (hardcover) |
    ISBN 9781797228631 (ebook)
Subjects: LCSH: Dwellings—Remodeling—United States. | Architects—
    United States. | Construction workers—United States. | Novogratz,
    Robert—Homes and haunts. | Novogratz, Cortney—Homes and haunts.
Classification: LCC TH4816 .N68 2024 | DDC 690.092—dc23/eng/20240506
    LC record available at https://lccn.loc.gov/2024010099

"

Life shouldn't be a
journey to the grave with
the intention of arriving
safely, but rather to skid
in broadside in a cloud of
smoke, thoroughly used up,
and loudly proclaiming,
'Wow! What a ride!'

—Hunter S. Thompson